Treasures of
ENFIELD

Discovering the Buildings of a London Borough

Edited by
Valerie Carter

This book is dedicated to the memory of Len Keeble (1941-97) who as leader of Enfield Preservation Society's Historic Buildings Group from 1978 until his death, did so much to protect listed buildings and stimulate an appreciation of the borough's architectural treasures.

Published by:
Enfield Preservation Society Ltd
Jubilee Hall, 2 Parsonage Lane, Enfield, Middlesex, EN2 OAJ

Registered charity No. 276451

ISBN 0 907318 16 9

British Library Cataloguing in Publication Data:
A catalogue record for this book is available from the British Library.

Designed by John Robey, Mayfield Books, Ashbourne DE6 2JR

Printed in Spain by Artes Graficas Elkar

Front cover: Forty Hall, Enfield (east front). Photo: Alan Bullock.
Rear cover (clockwise from top right): Chapel of Rest, Enfield Town; Queen Elizabeth Stadium, Donkey Lane; North Lodge, Whitewebbs Park; gateway, Enfield Grammar School; clock tower, Bramley Road Sports Ground. Centre: doorway detail, Garnault, Bulls Cross

Contents

Contributors to Treasures of Enfield

Illustrations

Edmonton Camera Club
Alan Bullock LRPS • Ron Degiorgio • Chris Demetriou LRPS
Alan Hollis • Peter Hunt • Gordon Fisher

Enfield Camera Club
David Abrahams • David James • Bren Neal ARPS • Steve Rudland
John Wallington • Andrew Walters • Rex Watts

Southgate Photographic Society
Ian Cameron Black • Frank Brzostowski ARPS • George Hillesdon
Peter Hodgkinson • Selva Kunalan LRPS • Christine M. Matthews
Dennis Poulter

Text

Enfield Preservation Society
Tim Bush • Alan Bullock • Valerie Carter • Matthew Eccleston
Clare Hansen • Pat Keeble • George Willox

Foreword

The London Borough of Enfield comprises two ancient parishes lying in the Lea Valley, Edmonton and Enfield. They are similar in shape and in nature, being oblongs, with their short eastern boundaries along the River Lea. Marshland in the east bordered the river. The marshes were drained early, to be transformed into rich meadow, the most valuable land in both villages. To the west lay a broad area of good arable where the great common fields were established. The land slopes gently up to the clay hills in the west where the early settlers left the heavy soil covered with its original forest.

The parishes, being only seven to ten miles from London, have always felt the influence of the great city. From medieval times they supplied it with hay to feed the horses and corn to feed the people. Travellers constantly passed through and some settled in the parishes. Settlements, with inns to service the horses, grew up along the Old North Road (Hertford Road); Edmonton Street lay near the Tottenham boundary, whilst the Edmonton village centre was at the junction of the roads to Hertford and Enfield Town. There were hamlets at Ponders End, at Green Street (Cocksmith's End) and at Enfield Wash (Horsepoolstones).

In Enfield the common arable fields extended from the Old North Road westward as far as Baker Street and the Town (Enfield Green). There lay the main settlement, with the church and the manor house on either side of the village green. In Edmonton the common arable land extended westward to the edge of the woodland, approximately the line of the Green Lanes. Within these common fields each peasant worked on a number of strips, according to rules laid down among the commoners. No dwellings could be built upon this common arable, for the rights of common were so vital to the cultivators that any attempt to encroach upon common land was met by implacable resistance. Even the wealthiest landowners seldom attempted such enclosure. Thus all the houses remained crowded together within existing settlements.

The woodland on the clay uplands in the west was early enclosed in both parishes. In Enfield, about 1136, it was ditched and fenced around and became a private hunting ground, known as Enfield Chase. Nevertheless the rights of common there, of those who occupied houses or land in either parish, were rigidly maintained, and so remained until the Chase was sold off in the late 18th century.

Nothing but the three lodges stood upon the Chase. In Edmonton the wood was early enclosed and extensively exploited as coppices, all privately owned. Two hamlets, Winchmore Hill and Southgate, developed among the woods. They housed the woodcutters, bark peelers and charcoal burners who toiled there for centuries. But following the Restoration of Charles II in 1660, these coppices came to be bought, one after the other, by wealthy Londoners, who established parks and built mansions there, like Arnos Grove, Grovelands and Southgate House, which still exist, and numerous others which have long since gone. Some of the families who purchased, particularly the Taylors at Grovelands, were so rich and owned so much land, that they were able, by their refusal to sell, to hold back housing developments in Southgate right through the 19th century, until 1902, creating their own private green belt.

Thus although the Great Northern built a railway line through the area in 1881, with stations at Palmers Green and Winchmore Hill, these stations remained with few customers until house building began early in the 20th century. Only at either extremity of the line, at Bowes Park and on the Bycullah estate near the Enfield terminus, did building begin in 1880.

The stories of Southgate and Edmonton had begun to diverge before this time. Edmonton was being submerged by the working class. The Act which empowered the Great Eastern to build the line through Tottenham and Edmonton to reach Enfield Town in 1872, obliged the company to issue twopenny workmen's returns to Liverpool Street Station (opened 1874). The population of Edmonton, including Southgate, was at this time 13,860. By 1901 the population of Edmonton alone had reached 46,899, while Southgate still had less than 15,000 people and remained rural. This striking disparity, both in social class and numbers, had created a demand in the wealthier part, Southgate, for independent local government and, despite the protests of the Edmonton Local Board, it was granted by Act of Parliament in 1881.

Working-class houses followed the line of the new railway through Edmonton. A number of roads were built off Silver Street, west of Pymmes Park, off Victoria Road near The Hyde and around the Brettenham Road area. Town Road and other roads off the Hertford Road, on both sides, were laid out by land companies. Church Street remained largely rural, except for the Hyde House estate. At Bush Hill Park, west of the railway, an elegant middle-class estate was begun after 1870. The station there did not open until 1880, following which working-class houses were built east of the line, to take advantage of the cheap workmen's fares.

Development at Enfield Town followed more slowly after the coming of the railways, and was more mixed. Great houses gave way to housing estates. The first to be built was Enfield New Town, on part of the grounds of the mansion at Bush Hill Park. It covered the area from London Road to Raleigh Road. Along Chase Side, Gordon House and Manor House were demolished and their grounds laid out for housing. Along Lancaster Road, Cedar House and the original Brigadier House, on the site now occupied by St Luke's Church, fell before the developers. The progress of building accelerated dramatically on both sides of Lancaster Road between 1898 and 1904; also on both sides of Southbury Road. Chase Side, Enfield formed a social dividing line between houses engendered by the Great Northern Railway to the west and the Great Eastern to the east.

Further housing development followed the coming of electric trams in 1908, all the way through Edmonton and east Enfield to Waltham Cross. Trams also assisted in the rapid growth of Palmers Green and its development as a shopping centre. But further north, on the way to Enfield Town,

development had to wait for the great housing boom of the 1930s.

Home building began very slowly after the First World War; just a few over-expensive council houses were built. The Cambridge Road was constructed in the 1920s, more to relieve unemployment than to move traffic. The east side of the road through Enfield was wisely given over to industry. Large tracts of land were being offered for building by 1929 and, for the first time, attempts were envisaged to control development through town planning.

In the western side of the borough a great new impetus to house building was created by the construction of the Piccadilly line extension in 1933. The western side of Southgate, which had remained rural, was now engulfed in middle-class dwellings. Stations were opened at Arnos Grove, Southgate, Oakwood and Cockfosters. Estates, well laid out and landscaped, covered virtually the whole area along the extension by 1939.

The open areas between Edmonton and Southgate and between eastern Enfield and the Town, formerly occupied by the common fields, were progressively built over in the Thirties. Firs Lane and Hedge Lane succumbed at last. Further east in Edmonton, the sort of houses even the working class might afford were being built. Estates along Latymer Road, Galliard Road and Nightingale Road seemed to grow daily, and were sold as soon as completed.

The respectable estate along Willow Road was laid out in 1934. The housing boom appeared unstoppable. Nothing, it seemed, could dam the tide of housing which threatened to spread north and west across the lands of Enfield Chase. But, in 1936 and 1937, Middlesex County Council purchased over four thousand acres as part of a Metropolitan Green Belt. With public vigilance this has so far restrained the tide of urbanization. That vigilance is only one of the self-imposed duties of the Enfield Preservation Society, which, as this book shows, is also concerned to foster an appreciation of Enfield's history and architectural heritage.

David Pam
May 2000

Acknowledgements

This book could not have been produced without the enthusiastic co-operation of photographers, historians and individuals from all parts of the borough. It demonstrates their pride in Enfield's history and architectural diversity, and forms a unique record of buildings in the London Borough of Enfield in the year 2000.

The project was begun in 1995 by Len Keeble, then leader of Enfield Preservation Society's Historic Buildings Group. Using the Department of the Environment schedule, he and his group decided which buildings should be included and invited local photographic societies to participate.

Progress came to a halt with his untimely death in 1997. However, the foundations had been so well laid that the group was eventually able to complete the book, albeit considerably later than originally intended.

We are indebted to many individuals. We are particularly grateful to Graham Dalling, the London Borough of Enfield Local History Officer, who provided much of the general historical information and checked the manuscript for inaccuracies; to Christine White, LBE Planning Officer with special responsibility for conservation, who dealt patiently with our queries and always supplied an informative answer; and to David Pam, the renowned local historian and author, who wrote the Foreword outlining the development of the London Borough of Enfield. Caroline Carter, Audrey Kirby and Sandra Knott stand out among others who have helped in various ways and we thank them, as well as those not mentioned by name, for their support.

The illustrations are a vital part of the book and we are indebted to those members of Enfield Camera Club, Southgate Photographic Society and Edmonton Camera Club whose splendid photographs bring the pages to life.

We are also grateful to the following individuals for the use of their copyright photographs: Peter Hodge, Southgate District Civic Trust (picture of Clarendon Arch); Geoffrey Bone, Southgate District Civic Trust (Ellington Court, Southgate); Stanley R. Smith, Enfield Preservation Society (Victorian fountain, Market Place, and Palace Gardens shopping precinct Enfield Town, Brecon House Gentleman's Row, The Goat public house). The photograph of A. H. Mackmurdo and his mother is reproduced by permission of William Morris Gallery, London E17, and that of Lamb's Cottage by permission of English Heritage.

The maps are reproduced from the 1999 Enfield Borough Street Plan Ordnance Survey Map by permission of Ordnance Survey on behalf of the Controller of Her Majesty's Stationery Office © Crown Copyright MC 100026981.

We are grateful to the London Borough of Enfield Information Services for permission to use the street plan and to reproduce the plan showing conservation areas in the borough.

The editor, on behalf of Enfield Preservation Society, would be grateful for additional information about any of the buildings (particularly dates of construction or alteration) for possible inclusion in future editions.

Valerie Carter

Architectural Time Chart

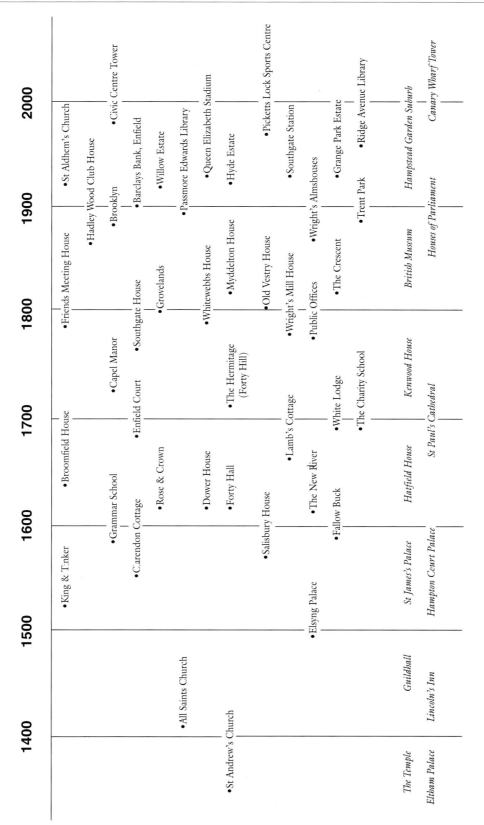

	1400	1500	1600	1700	1800	1900	2000

- King & Tinker
- All Saints Church
- St Andrew's Church
- Grammar School
- Carendon Cottage
- Broomfield House
- Capel Manor
- Enfield Court
- Southgate House
- Grovelands
- Friends Meeting House
- St Aldhem's Church
- Hadley Wood Club House
- Brooklyn
- Civic Centre Tower
- Barclays Bank, Enfield
- Willow Estate
- Passmore Edwards Library
- Rose & Crown
- Dower House
- Forty Hall
- Whitewebbs House
- Myddelton House
- Queen Elizabeth Stadium
- Hyde Estate
- Salisbury House
- The Hermitage (Forty Hill)
- Old Vestry House
- Picketts Lock Sports Centre
- Southgate Station
- Elsyng Palace
- Lamb's Cottage
- The New River
- Fallow Buck
- White Lodge
- The Charity School
- Wright's Mill House
- Public Offices
- Wright's Almshouses
- The Crescent
- Grange Park Estate
- Ridge Avenue Library
- Trent Park

The Temple
Eltham Palace
Lincoln's Inn
Guildhall
Hampton Court Palace
St James's Palace
Hatfield House
St Paul's Cathedral
Kenwood House
British Museum
Houses of Parliament
Hampstead Garden Suburb
Canary Wharf Tower

Introduction

The buildings around us are links with the past that bring local history to life. Every road has a story to tell, if one knows how to interpret the clues concealed in the bricks and mortar.

Enfield, Edmonton and Southgate have a gloriously rich and varied architectural heritage, including houses, pubs, schools, bridges and churches spanning every period from the twelfth to the twentieth century. To give the best of these buildings legal protection from demolition, unsympathetic alterations, or the destruction of their setting, the Department of the Environment has placed over 350 of them on the national List of Buildings of Special Architectural or Historic Interest.

Some buildings have been included for their design, decoration or craftsmanship, others for their historical significance or because they form part of an attractive group. They are listed under various grades:

Grade I — exceptional interest
Grade II* — important special interest
Grade II — special interest
Local Interest — on a list compiled by the local authority, with less statutory protection but subject to local policies.

Churches were originally listed by letter. Some have subsequently been re-listed:
A = Grade I
B = Grade II*
C = Grade II

How to use this Book

This book is designed to help readers take a fresh look at Enfield's buildings and discover the unexpected treasures to be found in every part of the borough.

The illustrations are grouped in seven main sections: each section covers a specific area and is accompanied by a location map. Dots on the maps indicate buildings referred to in the text, with an additional cross to show a church and PH for a public house.

The descriptions accompanying the illustrations include the name of the building, its address and listed status. Names of architects and designers are printed in italics.

Using the maps as a guide, the descriptions will lead the reader round each area, drawing attention to the astonishing variety of buildings, historic and modern, imposing and unpretentious, listed and unlisted, that give the London Borough of Enfield its special character.

The inclusion of a building in this book does not imply that it is open or accessible to the public.

Conservation Areas in the London Borough of Enfield

The 15 conservation areas in the London Borough of Enfield have been designated for their historic interest or architectural quality. The planning restrictions that come with conservation area status enable the Council to protect and enhance the special character and appearance of these areas. The areas are listed in order of their date of designation.

1. Enfield Town. Designated 1968, extended 1972, 1983, 1984, 1997. Area 64.5 Ha.
Originally designated to protect Gentleman's Row, then enlarged to cover the historic core of Enfield Town: St Andrew's Church, churchyard and Vicarage, White Lodge, the Market Place, Grammar School and playing fields. Now includes Holly Walk, Church Street, Raleigh Road, Cecil Road, part of Essex Road, Palace Gardens shopping precinct, Chase Green, Christ Church and part of Chase Side.

2. Forty Hill. 1968, extended 1987. 121.3 Ha. Rural and mostly in the green belt, but with a high proportion of listed buildings. Covers the two ancient villages of Forty Hill and Bulls Cross, extend-

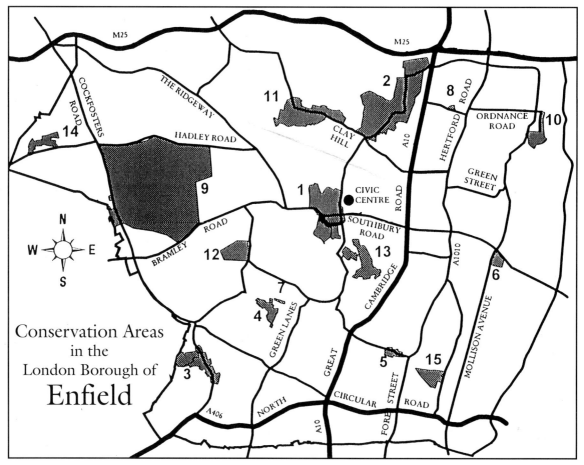

Conservation Areas
in the
London Borough of
Enfield

Plan provided by the London Borough of Enfield. By kind permission of Ordnance Survey © MC100026981

ing from Gough Park Cottage, the Goat, and village green, along the length of Forty Hill, over Maidens Bridge, through Bulls Cross and the grounds of Capel Manor to the New River. Forty Hall, the farm buildings, formal gardens and meadow are included.

3. Southgate Green. 1968, extended 1994. 31.7Ha.
The Green with surrounding houses and cottages, Christ Church, Parish Centre, cemetery, Walker sports ground, school, shops, Cherry Tree Inn – all the elements of a traditional village setting, still full of historic charm and character.

4. Winchmore Hill Green. 1968, extended 1994. 11.6 Ha.
The Green, Parish Church, Friends Meeting House, cottages in Harwoods Yard, cottages in Wades Hill – all the intact remnants of this once rural Middlesex village. The village green retains its character and remains a focus for the area, despite the intrusive traffic.

5. Church Street, Edmonton. 1970. 6.3 Ha.
All Saints Church and churchyard, Lamb's Cottage, Lamb's Institute and interesting C19 buildings. The heart of the ancient parish of Edmonton, still beating though ravaged by traffic in a densely built-up area.

6. Ponders End Flour Mills. 1970. 6.3 Ha.
The mill buildings, miller's house and adjacent meadows. One of the last remaining C19 industrial buildings in the Lea Valley. Surrounded by water meadows, the mill buildings, some weatherboarded, form a unique group and portray the changing techniques in flour milling over 200 years.

7. Vicars Moor Lane. 1970. 1.2 Ha.
Two groups of houses which have miraculously survived amidst the surrounding inter-war development, and remain a unique and well-maintained example of a C19 village street.

8. Turkey Street. 1972. 1.1 Ha.
Nos. 1-21 and 33-45 Turkey Street. Embracing properties on both sides of Turkey Brook, between two footbridges, the area was known some 200 years ago as Two Bridges. Though surrounded by development it remains surprisingly rural and is one of the area's few tangible links with the past.

9. Trent Park. 1973, extended 1990 and 1993. 386 Ha.
The whole of Trent Park Estate, including the mansion, country park, farm and golf course. Enlarged to include Victorian cottages at Nos. 303-345 Cockfosters Road, sports field in Chalk Lane, Christ Church and churchyard.

10. Enfield Lock. 1976, extended 1979. 13.2 Ha.
The lock, lock-keeper's house, waterways depot and surrounding open space, with cottages in Government Row, forming an interesting and attractive waterside group of historical importance.

11. Clay Hill. 1983. 53 Ha
From Stratton Avenue, up Clay Hill to the Fallow Buck and St John's Church, with part of Theobalds Park Road. Well spaced buildings extending into a semi-rural green belt area which is vulnerable to development.

12. Highlands. 1986. 21.7 Ha.
The former Highlands Hospital, N21. Designated to give the Council control of the site when it was redeveloped for housing. Remnants of the former fever hospital include well-built Victorian pavilions, set among mature trees on high ground with striking views across Trent Park.

13. Bush Hill Park. 1987, extended 1994. 28.7 Ha.
Spacious, well-designed and well-planted Victorian suburb based on Queen Anne's Place and Gardens, Dryden Road, Park Avenue, Wellington Road (northern end), Abbey Road and Private Road.

14. Hadley Wood. 1989. 13.4 Ha.
The 'village core' of the superior Victorian suburb of Hadley Wood, comprising Crescent East, Crescent West and the western section of Lancaster Avenue. Individually designed houses of style and substance.

15. Montague Cemeteries. 1996. 14.8 Ha.
The Tottenham Park and Jewish Cemeteries, on adjacent sites off Montague Road, N18, designated for their unique landscape qualities. The extensive Jewish Cemeteries comprise two contiguous burial grounds: one (opened 1884) run by the Western Synagogue, the other, under the aegis of the Federation Synagogue, opened in 1885 on land donated by the banker, Samuel Montague. Both contain fine marble and stone monuments.

Tottenham Park Cemetery, founded 1912 and privately owned, became overgrown with its chapel almost derelict until rescued by the Muslim community. Muslim monuments now predominate.

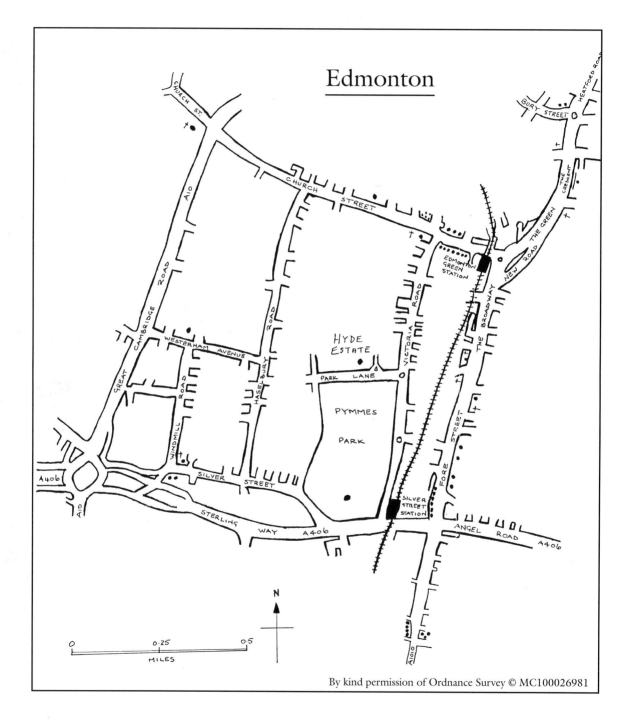

Edmonton

Upper **Edmonton** started life as a hamlet at the junction of Fore Street, Silver Street and Water Lane (now Angel Road). By the mid 1860s it had straggled along sufficiently to make a single-street village and meet its neighbour in Lower Edmonton. By the mid C19 the area was overcrowded and sanitary conditions, in the form of Pymmes Brook, a source of typhoid.

The North Middlesex Hospital still incorporates buildings from the old Edmonton Union Workhouse, built in Silver Street in 1842 to house the poor of six parishes. At this time horse buses ran every fifteen minutes along Fore Street to London. However, it was not until 1872 that a railway station was sited at Silver Street and workmen could take advantage of the cheap fares, with the subsequent development of working-class housing. Suburban development began in the mid C19 with the sale of Snells Park and continued until the early 1930s when little room was left for more.

In the late C19 the area had its own entertainment centre, the Theatre Royal, in Angel Road. This survived as a cinema until 1947 when it succumbed to the competition of one of the new breed of super-cinemas, the Regal, built in 1934 at the junction of Silver Street and Fore Street. Unfortunately, this too became a victim of changing trends and was demolished in 1986 to make way for a supermarket which has since closed.

In recent years the building of new shops and flats has, with limited success, attempted to lift the area's run-down appearance. A sculpture, pub name and plaque commemorate the area's claim to literary fame in the former Bell public house, immortalised in William Cowper's popular ballad 'The Diverting History of John Gilpin'.

No. 60 Fore Street. C18. Listed Local Interest

Nos. 62-64 Fore Street. C18. Listed Local Interest

Nos. 71 and 77 Fore Street. C18. Listed Local Interest. Look above and beyond the modern alterations and shop fronts to be reminded of the time when Edmonton provided a rural retreat for wealthy London merchants.

Nos. 67 and 69 Fore Street
(west side), **County Court,**
1940, Listed Local Interest

Angel Place, 183-195 Fore Street, Mid C18. Listed Grade II.

Remarkably intact composition of three blocks, all with two storeys and an attic linked by recessed one-window bays. (Somewhat compromised by rendered front of northern block). Tiled or slated mansard roofs with round-headed or flat dormers. Brown brick with cornice band and parapet, gauged red brick arches to sash windows, mostly with glazing bars. Six-panel doors (some altered) in Roman Doric doorcases with frieze, dentil cornice and open pediment and patterned fanlights. Periodically threatened by road improvement schemes (note loss of left outer bay from No. 183 and commemorative plaque on flank wall).

Nos. 236 and 238 Fore Street.
Early C18. Listed Grade II.
Pair of Georgian houses that in
spite of later alterations retain
sufficient features, including the
Roman Doric door surround
and wrought iron railings, to
reveal the original appearance.

Nos. 258 and 260 Fore Street.
Mid C18. Listed Grade II.
More Georgian houses, recently
renovated, each with three
storeys, five windows and a
basement. Moulded bands at
first and second-floor levels,
gauged brick segmental arches
to sash windows. Front doors
retain imposing Ionic
doorcases, medallion cornices
and pediments. No. 258 has
original wrought iron railings.

Nos. 258 and 260 Fore Street

Lower Edmonton

Once the principal settlement and administrative centre of Edmonton, **Lower Edmonton** dates from Norman times and these early beginnings can be seen in All Saints Church and the conservation area of Church Street. By early C19 this was a well established settlement at whose centre was the Green, where the main turnpike road from Hertford to London widened out. Here Salmon's Brook formed a large pool.

There was a half-hourly horse bus service to London and, by the end of the century, two stations linking Edmonton to Enfield Town and the City and a tramway along Fore Street. Attracted by cheap workmen's fares the area saw a vast working-class influx and by 1914 large areas of ribbon development. At its heart remained the Green flanked by a Town Hall, swimming pool, music hall, extensive shopping area and traditional street market.

The modern visitor will look in vain for these. Post-war depression and neglect wreaked havoc on Edmonton and by the 1960s the combination of dilapidated low-grade housing and an urgent need for more accommodation prompted a 'brave new world' solution. The heart was bulldozed away, to be replaced by roads, high-rise flats and shopping malls. Imagination is needed to recreate Lower Edmonton in its heyday but look carefully and you will find the remains of the old village, the Georgian houses and Victorian cottages. The market survives, though now enclosed, and plans are in hand to demolish some of the tower blocks (although not those on the Green) and rebuild the shopping centre.

Old Police Station, Fore Street (east side). 1990, *J. D. Butler*. Listed Grade II

Designed in LCC's Arts and Crafts manner, the building has an offset entrance between a bay window with stone architraved square-headed windows and a single similar window. The striking cornice breaks upwards into a central open pediment containing two pairs of square-headed dormers. Sympathetically converted into flats in the 1990s (note the residential infilling of former yard). Contrast the style with the modern replacement further down Fore Street.

Passmore Edwards Library

The Crescent

(Opposite, top) **Passmore Edwards Library,** Fore Street (west side) 1897 (extended 1931), *Maurice B. Adams.* Listed Grade II Formerly Edmonton Public Library, now a Sikh community centre. Symmetrical with an elaborate entrance bay, three different styles of window and original metal gates. Dutch scroll gables are complemented by Flemish bond red brickwork. Unusual corner buttresses with elaborate floral carving on the left one.

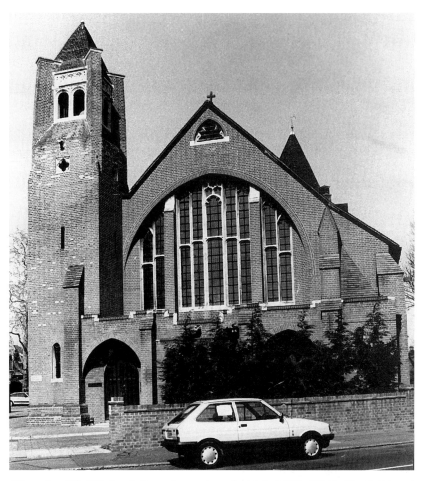

Church of St Michael, Bury Street (north side). 1901, *W. D. Caröe.* Listed Grade C (Group Value)
Very individual Arts and Crafts Gothic style in red brick with stone dressings, tiled roof, tower, elaborate east window and wide buttresses. Sensitively converted into flats after being made redundant in 1982.

(Opposite, bottom) **The Crescent,** Nos. 84 to 132 Hertford Road. Early C19. Listed Grade II (Group Value)
A reflection of the wealth and social pretensions of C19 Edmonton, this impressive terrace is built of brown brick with stucco ground floors, entablature and blocking course, three storeys and basement. Each house is two windows wide with a round, arched doorway and ground-floor window, first-floor french windows in round arched panels leading to balconies with cast iron railings.

Most windows are sashes with glazing bars. A few long first-floor casements remain, although some cornices are missing and have been replaced by plain cemented parapets. The centre and ends of the terrace are marked by giant stucco Corinthian pilasters which rise from first-floor level. Their absence on the left indicates that the block was never finished. This grandeur did not last and by 1974 the Crescent was described by a local councillor as a 'rat-infested warren, completely outdated and in this modern age simply not on'. He went on to suggest that he would like a tower block there instead. Fortunately, his opinion went unheeded and recently the Crescent has begun to regain some of its respect, although it is a pity that the original communal grass frontage has remained subdivided.

St Michael's Vicarage, Bury Street (north side). 1901, *W. D. Caröe*. Listed Grade II (Group Value) Red brick with tiled roof, large bay window, sashes under Tudor arches and two tiny round windows in the outer gables above the porch.

Nos. 20, 20A, 22, 22A Church Street. Early C19. Listed Grade II (Group Value)
Terrace of early cottages with part of the frontage converted in C19 into separate shops with stuccoed walls with parapet and tiled roof. Top storey retains recessed sash windows with glazing bars, replaced by modern window on ground floor. Compare door of No. 20 which has original six panels, with other glazed doors.

No. 24 Church Street.
C18. Listed Grade II
(Group Value)
Formerly Charity School
Mistress's house. A cottage
of red brick with renewed
pantiled roof. Two storeys,
sash window with glazing
bars in box frame on ground
floor (first-floor windows are
modern casements).
Doorway has architrave, cut
brackets, frieze and dentilled
cornice hood.

The Charity School, Church
Street (south side). 1784.
Listed Grade II (Group
Value)
Established in 1778 after
example of the Blue Coat
School in Tottenham. Brown
brick, gabled old tile roof
with one storey, two tall sash
windows with segmental red
brick arches. Above the
central round-arched
doorway in an arched niche is
a statuette of a pupil holding
an open book. The
inscription on the panel
below reads 'A Structure of
Hope, Founded in Faith and
Based on Charity, 1784'.
Now used as a public hall.

Lamb's Cottage, Church Street (north side). Late C17/early C18. Listed Grade II*

Timber-framed cottage of two storeys and an attic with slated mansard roof with dormer. C18 incised stucco front with parapet, sash windows with broad frames and glazing bars, door in older frame with cornice hood on brackets. The interior remains much as remodelled in the 18C with Georgian panelling, arches and open-string staircase. Originally known as Bay Tree or Walden's Cottage it was a private mental home in the C19 and later a Vestry Office. Renamed after its most famous occupant, the essayist Charles Lamb, who in 1832 chose to join his sister, Mary, who was a patient here. Early C19 **wrought iron railings** on brick wall and **gate** with overthrow, also listed.

(Opposite, top) **Post Office Sorting Office,** Nos. 44-48 Church Street. Early C20. Listed Local Interest. The **forecourt wall and railings** are also listed.

(Opposite, bottom) **Nos. 19 and 21 Church Street.** Early C19. Listed Grade II. Fine pair of Georgian houses, each with three storeys, attic and basement. Slated mansard roof with dormers. Walls of yellow stock brick finishing with a parapet wall. All the windows have double-hung sashes and the arch lintels are splayed brick. Gauged flat brick arches to windows, some with original glazing bars. The patterned fanlight in No. 19 indicates where the doorway was altered to a window. The doorway of No. 21 is obscured by the addition, later in the C19, of a porch.

The carved stone bench on the corner of Winchester Road commemorates Charles Lamb and John Keats, former residents of Church Street. This was the original site of the fire-station, now rebuilt further down Church Street.

Post Office Sorting Office

Nos. 19 and 21 Church Street

Nos. 35-41 Church Street. Early C19. Unlisted. Various houses which still retain original features, if somewhat obscured by modern additions, including a betting office.

Nos. 43-45 Church Street. 1840s. Unlisted. Contrast No. 43 with 45 which, having had sympathetic alterations, retains most of its original appearance with yellow stock brick, slate roof, architraves around windows, parapet walls, cornice and pediment over central door (unfortunately not as original).

(Opposite, top) **Charles Lamb Institute,** Church Street. 1908, *John S. Alder.* Listed Grade II Stone-faced building in style of Tudor college with large, stone mullion transomed windows and canted bays. The narrow doorway, now used as the main entrance, originally led to the one-bay dwelling section. A hanging sign advertises its present use.

Charles Lamb Institute

Church of All Saints, Church Street (south side). C15. Listed Grade B

The church, its churchyard and surrounding buildings and trees provide their own atmosphere and seclusion against the constant traffic. Although mainly C15, incorporated into the west wall is a fragment of the C12 masonry of the earliest church on this site. The tower is of ragstone rubble with battlemented parapet and angle buttresses with a stair turret. The north aisle and chancel were controversially refaced in stock brick in 1772. The south aisle, added in 1889, is of specked rubble with flint and stone panelling. The roofs are partly tiled, partly of green slate.

The essayist Charles Lamb and his sister Mary are buried in the **churchyard.** Adjoining the church are the **Alms Houses.** The original buildings were erected in 1679 and then rebuilt in 1754. These were demolished and rebuilt in 1903 and improved in 1960.

Nos. 71-77 Church Street. C19. Unlisted.
Two pairs of substantial four-storey houses which retain many of the original windows and some ironwork.

(Below) **Fire Station,** Church Street. 1941.
T. A. Wilkinson, Edmonton Architect's Department.
Unlisted.
Pleasingly symmetrical design with bowed ends.

(Opposite, bottom) **Pymmes Park, former garden walls.** Late C17/early C18. Listed Grade II.
Situated on the North Circular Road side of this extensive park, these walls are all that remain of the original Pymmes House and outbuildings. The site dates from the C14, its most famous owners being the Cecil family. Robert Cecil, first Earl of Salisbury, spent his honeymoon at Pymmes.

The estate was eventually acquired in 1897 by Edmonton Council and officially opened as a park in 1906. The house was subsequently demolished after being destroyed by fire during the Second World War. The walls now surround an attractive garden (note the mid C19 wall fountain with marble dolphin decoration). The garden can be visited during the summer months through a gate in the section of wall behind the former Health Clinic.

The wood sculpture on the grass in front of this building commemorates an ancient cedar tree destroyed during the widening of the road.

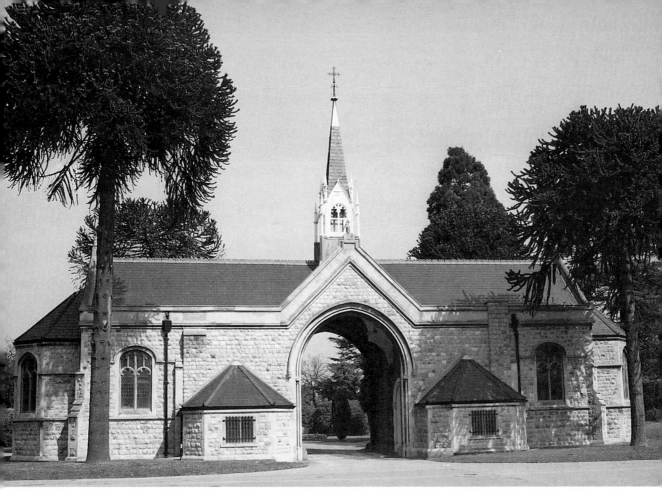

Edmonton Cemetery Chapels, Church Street (west side of A10). 1886-7. Unlisted. Stone chapels, each with an apse, linked by a wide carriage arch with spirelet above.

Pymmes Park, former garden walls

Church of St Aldhelm, Silver Street. 1903, *W. D. Caröe*. Listed Grade C.
Gothic style, very individually interpreted with Arts and Crafts influence. Red brick with dressing of stone and layered tiles, it has high pitched tiled roofs with a picturesque wood shingled spire and bell-cote.

Millfield House Entrance Lodge, Silver Street.
C19. Listed Grade II.

Simple, one-storey brick lodge with a low pitched slated roof, central chimney, sash windows with gauged brick arches in round-arched recesses. Unfortunately the symmetry is comprised by the glazed door replacing a window on the left of the central doorway.

Millfield House (formerly St David's Hospital), Silver Street. 1796. Listed Grade II*

Built as a country house, now linked at back to later hospital buildings and used as an arts centre. Made of stock brick with a stone-coped parapet, the three bays have slated roofs, one with a later raised mansard with dormer. Although the glazing bars have mostly been replaced, the sash windows retain their original style under flat brick arches (one has been blocked). The middle recessed bay is quite flamboyant, with a central window in a moulded architrave set in a wood pane, a stuccoed ground-floor centre section, Roman Doric columns and frieze and three round-headed, half-glazed doors in reeded architraves flanked by round-headed niches. Either side of this is a long, cast iron verandah with a swept roof.

Inside the house, there is an oval entrance lobby and overall stairwell with a striking curved staircase and glass dome. Doors and architraves are also curved to fit the shape of the wall. The house still retains several marble fireplaces including a handsome carved one in the right front room.

Houses on the **Westerham Estate,** Edmonton. Unlisted.

The Hyde Estate, Edmonton. 1920-22.
D. B. Niven. Unlisted.
Semi-detached houses, designed in the Arts and Crafts style, on the garden-city estate which Edmonton Urban District Council intended to extend from Victoria Road to Firs Lane and from Pymmes Park to Church Street. National financial constraints forced the Council to abandon their utopian scheme when only 232 houses had been completed out of a projected 2,000.

Eastern Enfield & Industrial Heritage

The eastern part of Enfield started as a series of hamlets strung out along the Hertford Road. The largest settlement was at Ponders End, with smaller ones at Green Street, Enfield Highway, Enfield Wash and Freezywater. The coaching trade was an early influence on development, especially after the improvement of the road following the Turnpike Act of 1713. The construction of the Lee Navigation in 1766, with locks at Ponders End and Enfield Lock, was an important stimulus to trade in the area.

Ponders End Station was opened in 1845. Transport links were subsequently improved by an electric tramway; this reached Ponders End in 1907 on its way to Waltham Cross and was extended along Southbury Road to Enfield Town four years later.

As the area grew, its close proximity to several large industries including brickworks, market gardening and the Royal Small Arms Factory contributed to the eventual blurring of boundaries and heavy density of housing.

Mans (formerly Ripaults Factory), Southbury Road, *c1930, A. H. Durnford*. Listed Grade II Rare surviving example of stuccoed, flat roof Art Deco 'decorated shed' with characteristic horizontal strip windows curving into the returns. Symmetrical, the building has a two-storey central block with one-storey wings, the centre and ends projecting slightly with rounded corners. In the centre is a rectangular tower with decorative chrome strips and a triangular window with an ogee rooflet. The central entrance has a projecting concrete canopy. Only remaining example from the once extensive light industrial area stimulated by the building of the Great Cambridge Road. Beautifully restored by present owners, although original colours were red and white.

Eastern Enfield & Industrial Heritage

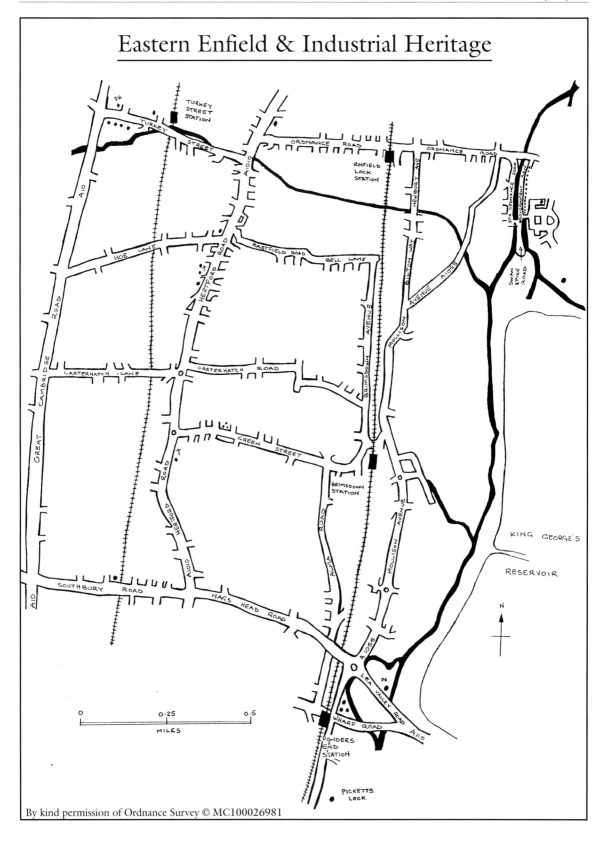

Church of St James, Hertford Road (east side). 1831, *W. C. Lockner.* Listed Grade C. Yellow brick with stone dressings, nave and integral west tower. The chancel was added in 1864 and the inside is completely altered with modern wood panelling and large windows.

Nos. 98 and 100 Green Street. C17. Listed Grade II
Probably originally one timber-framed building, now two houses. Two storeys with three windows in all. The roof, which has been renewed in machine tiles, has a massive ridge stack, now rough rendered. No. 100 is weatherboarded with modern casements and doors. The roof sweeps low behind. Listed, in spite of alterations, for its rarity value in this area. (Rear view illustrated.)

The White Horse Public House, Green Street (north side). C17. Listed Grade II
In spite of considerable alterations this remains a large timber-framed building with two storeys and attic, high pitched hipped tiled roof with three gabled dormers. This framing is exposed in the first-floor centre, tile-hung at the sides. The ground-floor plastering and porches are modern as are most of the casements, but one or two old ones remain.

Wright's Almshouses and forecourt walls, Nos. 346 to 356 Hertford Road. 1847. Listed Grade II. Symmetrical row of cottages, each with two storeys, one window and blank window panels above doors. The elaborate four-panel doors under their heavy stone cornice hoods and carved scrolled brackets imitate earlier C17 style. The stone tablet on the pediment above the four projecting centre bays contains the inscription 'These almshouses were erected and endowed by Mr Charles Wright of Enfield Highway for the support of six poor women'.

Nos 472 and 474 Hertford Road. Early C19. Listed Grade II. Attractive pair of houses with two storeys, wide proportions, a low pitched hipped slated roof with eave, rendered walls with incised lines. The ground-floor sash windows, doors and patterned radial fanlights are in round arched recesses.

The Bell Inn, Hertford Road (west side). Late C19. Listed Grade II.
Built in a style associated with early railway hotels, the right-hand extension to the ground-floor loggia with its imposing Roman Doric columns has been filled in to form an extra room. Attractive three-light sash windows on second storey.

Turkey Street

Although most of the buildings have suffered too many alterations to be considered worth listing, the part of Turkey Street which adjoins the Hertford Road, once known as 'Two Bridges', with its brook, cottages and trees, is one of the few places that still retains its rural character. The oldest properties probably date from the mid C18.

Nos. 120 and 122 Turkey Street. C19. Listed Grade II
Pair of cottages with wide doors and originally having Gothic casement windows, those on the ground floor under segmental arches. Only those on the upper storey of No. 120 remain, the bow window being a modern replacement.

Nos. 138 and 140 Turkey Street. Mid C18. Listed Grade II.
Pair of houses with stuccoed fronts, slated, double pitched, hipped roof comprising two storeys plus a basement. An elaborate Victorian porch marks the main entrance on the side elevation.

The Plough Public House, Turkey Street. Listed Local Interest. (Not illustrated.)

Anne Crowe's Almshouses, Almshouse Lane. Listed Local Interest.
Reached by a footpath from Turkey Street, this brick terrace of four separate houses was originally built on this site for the poor of the parish during the late C17. Later they were sold to Thomas Crowe, whose wife's name is commemorated through her legacy which provided for coal and repairs. Rebuilt 1893 by H. C .B. Bowles of Myddelton House.

No. 651 Hertford Road.
Early C19. Listed Grade II.
Two-storey three-bay villa with
low pitched, hipped slated roof
with deep eaves. Stock brick
with gauged brick arches, flat to
ground-floor windows and
round to doorway and to the
arched recesses in which door
and windows are set. Recessed
sash windows with glazing bars
in stucco-lined reveals. Modern
glazed door with blocked
fanlight.

Industrial Heritage

Enfield has a rich and ancient industrial heritage which has only recently begun to receive the attention it deserves. Much has already been lost, especially in the opportunities presented by the Royal Small Arms site. This area, known as Enfield Lock, developed alongside the expansion of the Royal Small Arms Factory in 1854. It formed a small, self-contained community with its own housing (Government Row), school, church, police station (now demolished) and hotel (now part of Rifles). A mill appeared on the 1867 Ordnance Survey map but only the mill pond remains. The oldest buildings in the area are contained within the Waterways Depot (not listed), which is currently being refurbished as housing and industrial units.

Bridge at Rammey Lock, Lee Navigation. 1835, *James R. Griggs*. Listed Grade II.
Canal bridge built by the trustees of the Lee Navigation. The plinths of banded stone and brick are all that remain of the original cast iron bridge and railings. (Not illustrated)

(Opposite, top) **No. 172a Government Row, Lock Keeper's House.** Unlisted.
Typical example of C19 canal architecture.

(Opposite, bottom) **Nos. 4-14, 18-28 Government Row,** Enfield Lock. 1854-8. Listed Grade II (Group Value).
Two-storey cottage row in Flemish bond brown brick with gabled Welsh slate roofs, gauged brick cambered arches over four-panelled doors and horned twelve-pane sashes. Built to house workers at the Royal Small Arms Factory. (Nos. 18-28 illustrated.)

No. 172a Government Row, Lock Keeper's House

Nos. 18-28 Government Row

Nos. 30-31 Government Row, Enfield Lock. Listed Local Interest.

Former Royal Small Arms Factory (now Island Village)

Remote, but with a good source of water power and transport links along the River Lea to the Royal Powder Mills at Waltham Abbey, in 1812 this site was identified as the ideal place to establish a government factory to ensure a regular supply of British-made quality armaments. The factory opened in 1816. Two huge cast-iron undershot wheels drove boring and turning benches, grindstones, polishing gear and rifling machines. Swords and bayonets were made as well as guns and musket barrels. Soon, its very isolation prompted the establishment of a whole community, as production continued even in peacetime with the recognition of the need to maintain a skilled workforce.

The elegant buildings we see today date from the greatest period of expansion at the commencement of the Crimean War, when in 1854-6 the Ordnance Board authorised the expenditure of a quarter-of-a-million pounds on the swift building of a new small arms manufactory equipped with the latest American mass-production machinery. By 1859 over 1,200 men were employed and around 100,000 weapons a year produced, the pride of these being the Enfield Rifle.

The workforce increased to 2,400 after the introduction of steam power in 1886 and the factory consolidated its position as the principal supplier of weapons to the army with the Lee Enfield rifle, designed in 1895. The world-famous 1902 Short Magazine Lee Enfield remained in production for fifty years. Enfield's importance is also seen in the 'EN' within the Bren and Sten guns, both produced here.

The residential development created on the site, although retaining a few of the most historic buildings and reinstating some of the internal waterways, ignores and diminishes the world-wide significance of the area.

Machine Shop and attached range, Royal Small Arms Factory, Ordnance Road. 1854-58. Listed Grade II

The machine shop was the largest and most important of the new buildings erected on the site by the Board of Ordnance during the C19 and was regularly opened to the public. Its great size was designed to facilitate the entire production process in one area of neatly aligned machinery. One storey with a 23-window range, the façade is Italianate in style with polychromatic brickwork of yellow with red brick dressings and alternating red and yellow brick voussoirs to arches and Welsh slate roofs. At the centre is a three-storey clock tower and belfry. Beneath a hipped roof, this has windows with glazing bars set in semi-circular arches linked by red brick impost course, red brick corbelling beneath frieze of diaper work and a moulded stone cornice.

Water Tower House, Pump House and Retort House, King George Pumping Station, Swan and Pike Lane (east side). Opened 1913, *William Booth Bryan* for Metropolitan Water Board. Listed Grade II.

No public access, can be viewed from Sewardstone footpath. Imposing Edwardian Baroque style with English bond red brick and limestone dressing.

The **Pump House** has corner turrets but unfortunately the diamond latticed windows have been removed. Originally housed five cast-iron gas pumps housed in deep brick-lined pits. A unique design by H. A. Humphrey and the first example of their type in the world, each pump was capable of raising 40 million gallons of water each day from the Lee Navigation into the King George Reservoir. The

Retort House was used for storing gas, made from anthracite, before it was passed into the Pump House, which was last used in 1968.

NB. Rather than going back to the road, the next building can be viewed by returning to the River Lea towpath and walking south to Ponders End Lock.

Wright's Flour Mills, Wharf Road, Ponders End. (No public access but can be viewed from road or the footbridge adjacent to the Lodge). One of the last remaining C18 industrial sites in the Lee Valley and Enfield's oldest industrial working building. There was a mill here in the C16. The water meadows surrounding the Mill provide an unexpectedly rural setting for this interesting group of buildings which reflect in their different designs and materials the changing techniques in flour milling over 200 years. Their survival is due to the policy of successive generations of the Wright family, who have maintained the attractive façades whilst converting the interiors to more efficient production methods.

(Below) **Lodge Cottage** at entrance. Early C19. Listed Local Interest.

House to east of Old Mill Building. Late C18. Listed Grade II.
Two-storey and attic building with mansard slate hipped roof with C18 flat-topped sash dormers. The central doorcase has an open pedimented porch on Doric columns. (Not illustrated.)

Barn Timber-framed, weatherboarded barn, probably early C18. Half-hipped roof part tiled, part slated. (Not illustrated.)

Lodge Cottage, Wright's Flour Mills

Mill Owner's House

Old Mill Building

(Opposite, top) **Mill Owner's House.** Late C18. Listed Grade II.

Brick house with mansard attic, large bays with C19 sashes and C18 dentil cornices and a central open-pedimented Tower of the Winds columned porch, leading onto a doorway with a round-headed ornamental fanlight.

(Opposite, bottom) **Old Mill Building,** C18 with alterations. Centre block is the flour mill, upper part is weatherboarded with a projecting sack hoist. Modern loading-bay extension.

The Old Mill Building, the Mill Owner's House, the house to east of Old Mill Buildings and the Barn form a working group, a very rare survival in London.

(Below) **Former Well Station** of Thames Water Authority, (now Navigation Inn), Lea Valley Road, Ponders End. 1899, *W. B. Bryan.* Listed Grade II. Picturesque building in vernacular revival style, sympathetically converted in 1995. Half-timbered attic storey has roughcast filling and C17 style casements and rests on long timber brackets. Main floor has large square-headed windows, mullioned and transomed, which almost touch and floor-length, round-headed glazed openings. An original large door in the right return rises to height of jetty.

Former Well Station

UCI Cinema, Picketts Lock, Lea Valley Leisure Centre, Meridan Way. 1993, *Fitzroy Robinson & Partners.* Unlisted. A later addition to the first sports and leisure centre (1973) developed by the Lee Valley Regional Park Authority.

Forty Hill, Bulls Cross, Whitewebbs & Clay Hill

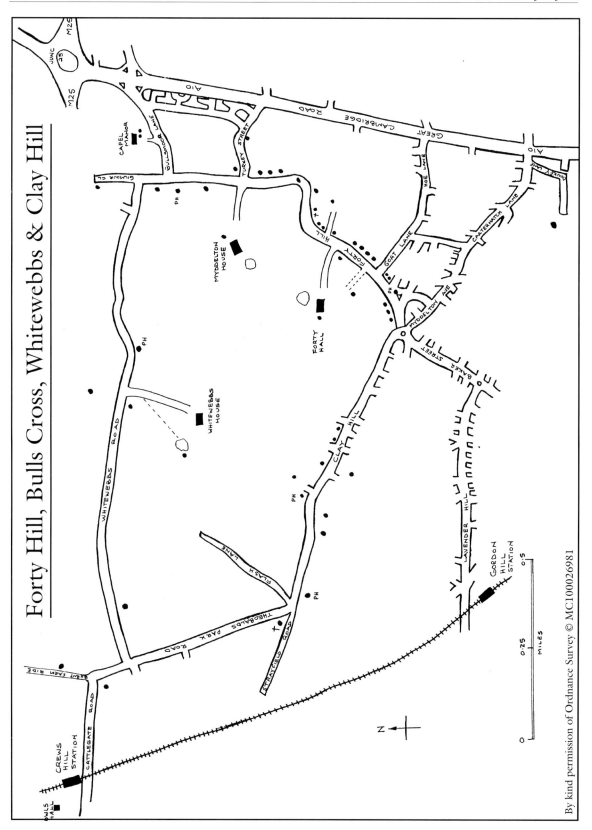

Forty Hill, Bulls Cross, Whitewebbs & Clay Hill

Forty Hill, Bulls Cross, Whitewebbs and Clay Hill form one of the most attractive rural areas in Enfield. Before 1570 there were settlements in Forty Green (now Forty Hill), in Bulls Cross Lane (Bulls Cross) with two clusters in Whitewebbs Lane and more cottages in what was known as Bridge Street, in Clay Hill near the Rose and Crown.

In the sixteenth century Forty Hill was dominated by Elsyng, Sir Thomas Lovell's palace, which covered most of the meadow in Forty Hall park, leading down to the Turkey Brook. The palace, which originated as a timber-framed structure, was replaced by a large brick building *c*1487, after which it was frequently visited by royalty. It was demolished soon after 1656 but by then the area had begun to attract the London gentry. Forty Hall had already been built, to be followed by other fine houses over the next hundred years or so: The Dower House, The Hermitage, Worcester Lodge, Longbourn, Elsynge House, Whitewebbs, Capel House, Bramley House, Myddelton House, with attendant cottages, inns and more modest dwellings, many of which are still standing.

Perhaps because there were no easy transport links with Enfield Town, the area remained mainly rural until well after the First World War. The Bridgen Hall estate, stretching between Goat Lane and Carterhatch Lane, had been sold in 1868. But although Garnault Road, Bridgenhall Road, Layard Road, Russell Road and St George's Road had been laid out, sales were slow and some plots remained vacant well into the 1930s.

Two railway stations (Crews Hill and Gordon Hill, both opened 1910), a bus service into Enfield and construction of the Great Cambridge Road (A10) in 1924 stimulated housing development which, had it not been for the 1939 green belt legislation, could soon have engulfed the whole area. Crews Hill remains a prime target for developers, although the nursery gardens which were its mainstay until the 1970s have been replaced by thriving garden centres. Steadily increasing traffic since the opening of the M25 in 1984 is another threat to the rural charm of the area.

Since the Second World War, major council estates have been built north of Hoe Lane and between Turkey Street and Bullsmoor Lane.

Gates and brick walls to Gough Park, Forty Hill. Early C18. Listed Grade II. Fine ornamental wrought iron gates and railings, all that now remains of a more extensive entrance to the residence, demolished in 1899, of Richard Gough FSA, FRS (1735-1809). Some of the walls north of the modern Gough Park Cottage in Clay Hill may date from 1774 when Gough came into the original property.

Cottage Place

The Hermitage

(Opposite, top) **Cottage Place,** 70-76 Forty Hill. 1833. Listed Grade II.

Four artisan cottages, once part of a much longer terrace. Local yellow brick with red brick dressings, stylish ground-floor windows set in recessed arches. Note the blank window panels over doors on party walls.

(Opposite, bottom) **The Hermitage and attached stable building,** 78 Forty Hill. 1704. Listed Grade II*.

Glorious house in dark red local brick, acknowledged as a perfect example of its date. Steep hipped roof with dormers above dentilled cornice, handsome early C18 door surround with rusticated Doric pilasters. The irregular chimneys and off-centre entrance suggest an older house remodelled and the back is indeed timber-framed work of the early C17. Inside, front rooms have original panelling, back rooms have C17 square panelling. Weatherboarded timber-framed stable building attached on left.

The Dower House

The Dower House and Atherton House, Forty Hill. Early/mid C17. Listed Grade II.

Up a drive on the west side of Forty Hill, the **Dower House** was part of Forty Hall estate until 1787 and was known as The Gables until the early 1900s. Now converted to two dwellings, the attractive L-shaped house was much altered and refaced in the C18. Dower House has east front with two gables and early C19 long casement windows on ground floor with three more gables on north front. In the early 1970s a painted mural *c*1600 was uncovered on a chimney breast in a panelled room on the ground floor. **Atherton House** has an early C19 stuccoed façade with angle pilasters on its north side.

Forty Hall, Forty Hill, 1629. Listed Grade I.
An imposing **Entrance Gateway** (c1800, Listed Grade II) comprising six tall piers of rusticated stone, the central piers decorated with garlands, gives access to Forty Hall and the extensive landscaped estate.

Left of the entrance, note the gabled **Lodge** (c1903, *Sidney M. Cranfield.* Unlisted). All the timber work is oak, with the Bowles family crest carved on the front of the house.

The square, red brick Forty Hall was built from 1629-1636 for Sir Nicholas Raynton, who became Lord Mayor of London in 1632. Three compact storeys, with one of the earliest hipped roofs of its kind, the house has undergone many changes inside and out. Bought by James Meyer in 1799 and

retained by his descendants until 1895, it was then sold to Henry Carington Bowles, the owner of Myddelton House *(qv).* He bought it for his eldest son, who as Colonel Sir Henry Bowles served as Enfield's MP, was its representative on Middlesex County Council and was prominent in local affairs until his death in 1943. Forty Hall was inherited by Sir Henry's grandson Derek Parker Bowles who, when his health failed, sold the house and estate to Enfield Council in 1951 for £43,000.

The house is now a museum and art gallery. Inside, some of the original decoration survives, including several splendid plaster ceilings and one panelled room, also a screen with early classical motifs in the dining room. Much of the other decoration is C18.

Screen wall, gateway and north pavilion, Forty Hill. 1630. Listed Grade I.

To the west of the house, a rectangular courtyard is approached through high wrought-iron gates set in an exuberant, embattled wall with small pavilions at either side. The courtyard is flanked by the former **Stable Range** (C17, Listed Grade II) converted into a banqueting suite.

Barns (C17, Listed Grade II) round an outer courtyard were restored in 1998.

Capel Manor Centre has a long lease of the farm-land on the estate, together with the barns and the farm buildings west of the house. The rest of the grounds, including the walled former kitchen garden are open to the public. The park and gardens are listed Grade II in the Department of the Environment register of historic parks and gardens. Beneath the meadow north of the house lie the remains of **Elsyng Palace,** occupied by Sir Thomas Lovell from 1492 and used as a royal residence from the mid-1500s until its demolition *c*1656.

The Goat. 1932. *A. E. Sewell.* Unlisted. Dominating the village green and standing near the site of the old forge and village pond, this Mock Tudor public house is one of a series designed for Truman Hanbury between the wars. Note the ornate chimneys (modelled on those at Hampton Court) and elaborately carved bargeboards.

Canister Lodge, 29 Forty Hill. Late C18. Listed Local Interest.

Thin, late Georgian villa with four giant arches and later porch, said to resemble a tea canister.

Worcester Lodge, 35 Forty Hill. *c*1704.
Listed Grade II.
Classic five-bay two-storey house which lost most of its front garden when Forty Hill was widened *c*1911. Red brick with first-floor band, high pitched tiled roof with dormers and dentilled eaves cornice. Elegant pedimented door frame.

The old **Goat House,** 37 Forty Hill. C17. Unlisted.
(Not illustrated.)
On the corner of Goat Lane, this is the former Goat Inn, once thatched and weatherboarded.

(Right) **Forty Hill House,** Forty Hill. Early C19.
Listed Grade II.
Three imposing storeys and basement, yellow stock brick with stone-coped parapet concealing the roof. Ground-floor windows set in arched recesses. Handsome pedimented porch with fluted Doric columns. Now converted into flats.

Longbourn

Elsynge House and Cottage

(Opposite, top) **Longbourn,** Forty Hill. *c*1720. Listed Grade II.

A long house with five bays, originally a farmhouse. Stucco and north wing added around 1800. Southern extension, porch and entrance door are Victorian.

(Opposite, bottom) **Elsynge House and Elsynge Cottage,** Forty Hill, House early C18, Cottage late C18. Listed Grade II.

Interesting house of several periods, unified by front of brown brick and notable for its many attractive windows. Finely detailed Venetian windows with fluted friezes on ground floor, all first-floor windows are lengthened lunettes. Now two dwellings. **Elsynge House** was once the home of Cuthbert Whitaker, author of a *History of Enfield* (1911).

(Below) **Clock House Flats Nos. 1-9.** Forty Hill. C19. Listed Local Interest.

Massive stuccoed house with vermiculated quoins, now divided into flats with extensions at both ends. The back of the house is less forbidding, with two-storey rounded bays enclosing tall curved windows.

Clock House Flats

Clock House Nursery Cottage

Waltham Cottage

(Opposite, top) **Clock House Nursery Cottage,** Forty Hill. C19. Listed Local Interest*

At the end of the lane to Clock House Nursery, cottage with distinctive latticed windows and decorative bargeboards. Modern porch and side extension.

(Opposite, bottom) **Waltham Cottage,** Forty Hill. Last quarter C18, restored C20. Listed Grade II. Red brick front with parapet, gauged flat yellow brick arches to recessed sash windows with glazing bars. Large modern extension at back.

Sparrow Hall, Forty Hill. C18. Listed Grade II.

Two storeys with attic, high pitched roof and three flat dormers; stables and coach house at rear. Originally a timber farmhouse, refronted in brick 1802. Gauged near-flat brick arches to recessed sash windows with glazing bars. Canted bay added to ground floor, with further extensions on right and at rear, between 1835 and 1840 after the house became the vicarage to Jesus Church. Sold by the church and reverted to original name in 1963.

Sparrow Hall

Jesus Church, Forty Hill. 1835, *Thomas Ashwell*. Unlisted.

Modelled on Holy Trinity, Tottenham and constructed by Thomas Ashwell, a Tottenham carpenter and builder, at the expense of Christian Meyer, then owner of Forty Hall. Grey brick with paired lancets to aisles and clerestorey. The four corner finials on the roof became unsafe in 1913; two were rebuilt and the other two were adapted to form the war memorial in front of the church. Dry rot closed the church from 1982-84 while the roof was reconstructed in modern materials.

(Opposite, top) **Forty Hill School.** 1851. Listed Local Interest.

Single storey with attached two-storey teacher's house. Modernised and extended, but retaining some original features including the attractive latticed windows, this is the oldest junior school still in use in Enfield.

(Opposite, bottom) **Maidens Bridge.** 1761, rebuilt 1968. Unlisted.

The upper parts of the bridge over the Turkey Brook were rebuilt in 1968 after extensive damage by a lorry. A bridge was recorded here in medieval times with an adjacent water mill.

Forty Hill School

Maidens Bridge

Nos. 4 and 5 Maidens Bridge Cottages

Infants School, Maidens Bridge

(Opposite, top) **Nos. 4-7 Maidens Bridge Cottages,** Bulls Cross. C19. Listed Grade II.
Picturesque group of cottages which retain their rural character despite some modernisation.
No. 7, early-mid C19, of two storeys, has roof renewed in late C19 fancy tiles and a rounded arch to the central doorway. Blocked first-floor window and fanlight. **Nos. 4 & 5,** mid C19, one storey with attic, was possibly the teacher's house for the little school next door. Note the wood hood-moulds to the small-paned casements in chamfered reveals. **No. 6,** early-mid C18 with alterations (rear extension and raised roof) has two old end chimneys, the southern one rendered.

(Opposite, bottom) **Infants School,** Maidens Bridge. 1848. Listed Local Interest.
Tiny one-storey, single classroom with blank gable end to road and gabled porch with Tudor arched entrance. Both gables stone-coped. Built by James Meyer of Forty Hall, used as a school until his death in 1894. Later used as a Scout Hall, now part of **No. 3 Maidens Bridge Cottages.**

(Below) **Garnault,** Bulls Cross. *c*1860. Listed Local Interest.
Large, somewhat intimidating Italianate house in grey brick under slate roof. Six rounded arch windows with keystones to ground floor, with central round-headed porch. Birthplace of B. J. T. Bosanquet, Middlesex & England cricketer who invented the 'googly' in 1903 while playing for England against Australia. The old course (now dry) of the New River runs through the garden. The building has a striking resemblance to Clay Hill House.

Garnault

Myddelton House, Bulls Cross. 1818. *George Ferry & John Wallen*. Listed Grade II.

Headquarters of the Lee Valley Regional Park Authority. Plain but dignified house of two-and-a-half storeys in stock brick. Projecting central porch with Ionic columns. Later three-story right wing has round bow through two floors, with pilasters and entablature. The lifelong home of E. A. Bowles (1865-1954) youngest son of Henry Carington Bowles.

E. A. Bowles who was vice-president of the Royal Horticultural Society and a famous plantsman, laid out the garden, parts of which survive, and described it in a renowned trilogy of books. The garden, which is open to the public, is listed Grade II on the national register of historic parks and gardens. It contains the stone **Market Cross** on four buttressed piers with flying buttresses above (listed Grade II) which stood in Enfield Market Place 1826-1904. Other listed items: iron bridge dated 1832 erected by the New River Company over the old course of the river, now dry, and a lake terrace with stone ornaments and balustrading from Old London Bridge. The tall C18 brick wall east of the garden is also listed.

Market Cross, Myddelton House

Stable Block to north of Myddelton House. Early C19. Listed Grade II. Satisfying brick building with two-storey round-headed archway and inset porch, tympanum of arch filled with radiating panelling. Circular clock turret of wood decorated with pilasters and two circular clock dials. Original dome and weathervane.

Bridge over New River, Turkey Street. 1827 Listed Grade II.
Cast by Priestfields Iron-works, near Bilston. Segmental arch with open spandrels and raised keyblock, bearing date. Segmental-arched railings have circular bars with squared tops and bottoms; and square, panelled end-columns with pyramidal caps.

Gate House, West Lodge and East Lodge, Turkey Street, Bulls Cross. C18. Listed Grade II. Two-storey C18 house with lower early C19 left wing of two storeys and linked one-storey pavilion at right. Stuccoed parapet front probably mid C19. Now divided into three dwellings. To the west of Gate House, the red brick wall (north part late C17/early C18, south part late C18) is also listed.

(Below) **Myddelton Farm House**, Bulls Cross. C19. Listed Local Interest. Pleasing brick house flanked by outbuildings. Note the striking fanlight over front door. This straight stretch of road follows the line of the Roman Ermine Street which led out of London.

Myddelton Farm House

(Opposite) **The Pied Bull,** Bulls Cross. C17. Listed Grade II. Flanked by cottages in the ancient hamlet of Bulls Cross, the two-storey building looks earlier than C17. One-storey left extension, projecting one-storey gabled right wing. Rendered first floor oversailing on curved brackets. High pitched tiled roof with eaves broken by raised C20 first-floor windows. Windows on weather-boarded ground floor are C18 sliding sashes. Large C20 extension at rear.

The Pied Bull

The Orchards, Bulls Cross. Early C18. Listed Grade II.
Two storeys with one-storey left extension. Until 1924 this was an inn called the Spotted Cow, competing for custom with the Pied Bull.

Capel Manor

(Opposite, bottom) **Capel Manor,** Bullsmoor Lane. Mid-late C18. Listed Grade II. Imposing brick house of seven bays with side wings and gambrel roof of graduated slates with five flat dormers. Moulded brick cornice with stone-coped parapet. Good timber porch with Corinthian columns. Similar rear (north) elevation but with Roman Doric central porch. Some rich interiors with a splendid inlaid floor and much carving and panelling, dating from 1902 when house was remodelled in reproduction Restoration style.

Now a horticultural centre with extensive specimen and trial gardens open to the public.

Stables and former coach-house, Capel Manor. Late C19. Listed Grade II.
Splendid U-shaped range of red brick buildings surmounted by square brick tower with clock face on each side, pyramidal roof and 1954 weathervane depicting one of the prizewinning Clydesdale cart-horses bred by Colonel Medcalf, the last private owner of Capel Manor. Original fittings of exceptionally high quality in stables.

Front porch, Capel Manor

Bulls Cross Lodge

North Lodge

(Opposite, top) **Bulls Cross Lodge,** Gilmore Close. Mid C19. Listed Grade II.

Picturesque L-shaped lodge with stuccoed walls. High pitched roofs banded in plain and fishscale tiles with bargeboarded gable ends. Almost destroyed by fire in 1992; Enfield Council received a Civic Trust award for its sensitive restoration.

(Opposite, bottom) **North Lodge,** Whitewebbs Road. C19. Listed Grade II.

Delightful Victorian *cottage orné* at entrance to Whitewebbs Park. High pitched roof of fishscale tiles, richly decorated bargeboards and gable ends. Stuccoed, with interesting window detail. Saved from demolition by Enfield Preservation Society, 1971.

Whitewebbs House, Whitewebbs Road. C18, remodelled C19. Listed Local Interest.

Deep inside Whitewebbs Park, the house built for Dr Abraham Wilkinson in 1791 was given the look of a French chateau in 1881 when *Charles Stuart Robinson* added a wing and embellishments including a large curved pediment to the west front. Whitewebbs estate was bought by the local authority in 1931. The house, for many years an old people's home, is now a pub/restaurant. The former stable block (now a golf clubhouse) and garden walls are also listed.

Conduit House, Whitewebbs Road. C17. Listed Local Interest.

Small, square brick building beside the lake in Wilkinsons Wood, Whitewebbs Park, now in some disrepair and almost hidden by bushes. Probably the pump chamber or well-head for the water supply to Whitewebbs House. Possible Tudor foundations.

Conduit House

(Above) **The King and Tinker,** Whitewebbs Road. Early C17. Listed Grade II. Local legends surround the early days of this rural inn, in which roughcast walls and high pitched tiled roofs unify C18 and C19 alterations. Some C18 sash windows with glazing bars under heavy hoodmoulds. Modern square bay in centre.

Whitewebbs Farmhouse, Whitewebbs Road. C17. Listed Grade II. (Not illustrated.) Almost opposite the King and Tinker, the red brick farmhouse with hipped roof and three dormers had its front renewed mid C19.

Pumping Station

Glasgow Stud Farmhouse,
Burnt Farm Ride. Mid C17.
Listed Grade II.
Up a narrow lane at Sander's
corner, junction of Theobalds
Park Road and Cattlegate
Road. Wide brick-built house
with twin gables back and front
with ridges linked by a central
cross-ridge. Rendered front and
porch (C19). Sun insurance
plaque dated 1784.

London Aquatic premises,
Cattlegate Road. Early C18.
Listed Local Interest.
From the early 1700s this was
the Plough Inn. It became a
private dwelling in 1937 when
the new Plough was built few
yards away.

Footbridge, Theobalds Park
Road. Early-mid C19. Listed
Grade II. (Not illustrated.)
Ornamental brick footbridge
with very wide single seg-
mented arch span, at west end
of lane in Whitewebbs Wood.

(Opposite, bottom) **Pumping Station,** Whitewebbs
Road. 1898. Listed Local Interest.
Whitewebbs Museum of Transport. Typical Metropolitan Water Board architecture. Red brick with
long arched windows and pedimented porch, built
to supply the New River loop (now dry) which ran
through Whitewebbs.

Owls Hall

Church of St John the Baptist

(Opposite, top) **Owls Hall,** off Cattlegate Road (north side). Early-mid C19. Listed Grade II. Two-storey stuccoed villa with low-pitched hipped slate roof. Casement windows in moulded architraves. Stone front terrace up four steps with curved side walls. Rounded bow on right return.

(Opposite, bottom) **Church of St John the Baptist,** Clay Hill. 1857. *J. P. St Aubin.* Listed Grade II. Yellow brick with lively red and blue brick decoration. Shingled flèche on roof to west end of nave. Three-bay nave, aisleless, with lower chancel of two bays. Set of fine stained glass windows by *Heaton, Butler & Bayne.*

The Fallow Buck Inn, Clay Hill. C16/17. Listed Grade II. Shallow U-shaped weatherboarded building with gabled side projections and rendered right return. Early C19 sash windows with glazing bars on ground floor. C19 one-bar casements on first floor.

(Right) **South Lodge,** Whitewebbs Park (off Clay Hill, north side). Early-mid C19. Listed Grade II.
Pretty one-storey L-shaped gate lodge to Whitewebbs Park, similar in style to North Lodge,

Whitewebbs Road. Projecting porch with gables and fancy large brands. Ornamental crenellated chimneys.

Clay Hill Lodge, Clay Hill (south side). Early-mid C19. Listed Grade II
Ornamental lodge with central chimney. First floor pebble-dashed. Loggia, with hipped slated roofs and wood posts, all around rendered ground floor. Attractive ground-floor pointed windows with Gothic tracery.

Clay Hill House, Clay Hill (south side). 1853. Unlisted. (Not illustrated.)
Standing back from the road, this large house, built in Italianate style in pale grey brick with arched windows, was once the home of Joseph Toms (of Derry & Toms).

The Rose & Crown, Clay Hill. C16/17. Listed Grade II.
Long, picturesque timber-framed building with early C18 brick front, now painted white. High pitched tiled roof with gabled dormers. The early C19 two-storey right part with slated roof was used for many years as a shop. The building faces Hilly Fields Park, formerly farmland, bought by the local authority in 1911.

(Above) **Bramley House,** Clay Hill. 1750.Listed Grade II. In brown brick with red brick dressings, cornice band and stone-coped parapet. The original central section of five windows has left extension of 1881 and right extension of 1926, both in roughly similar character. Rear elevation early C19 with three wrought-iron balconies at first-floor level. Was a hospital for some years, now flats.

Telephone kiosk, type K6, Clay Hill near jnct. Browning Road. 1935 *Sir Giles Gilbert Scott*. Listed Grade II. (Not illustrated)
The model originally known as the 'Jubilee' kiosk. Cast iron with domed top, horizontal glazing bars and good proportions.

The brick **stable building** behind Bramley House is listed Local Interest.

Little Pipers

The Firs

(Opposite, top) **Little Pipers,** Clay Hill. Early C19. Listed Grade II.

Shielded by a wall and bushes and set in an extensive garden with listed walls, the attractive early C19 stuccoed exterior encases a much older house, probably early C18 with added wings. Bargeboards to central gables, hoodmoulds to windows in main block.

(Opposite, bottom) **The Firs,** Clay Hill. Early C19. Listed Grade II.

Two-storey central block with seven windows and set-back side wings. Stuccoed with cill bands; entablature and blocking course to main block. Modern central entrance in open-pedimented Ionic porch. Heavy moulded, rusticated architraves to ground-floor windows.

Pavilion at Queen Elizabeth Stadium, Donkey Lane. 1930s. *Frank Lee.* Unlisted.

One of Enfield's few buildings in the 1930s 'modern' style, designed by the architect/engineer for Enfield Urban District Council. Construction, suspended on outbreak of war in 1939, resumed in 1950. The streamlined sports pavilion with curved ends, projecting flat roofs and a café at the east end was opened in 1953. Refurbished and renamed in 1977 on the Queen's Silver Jubilee.

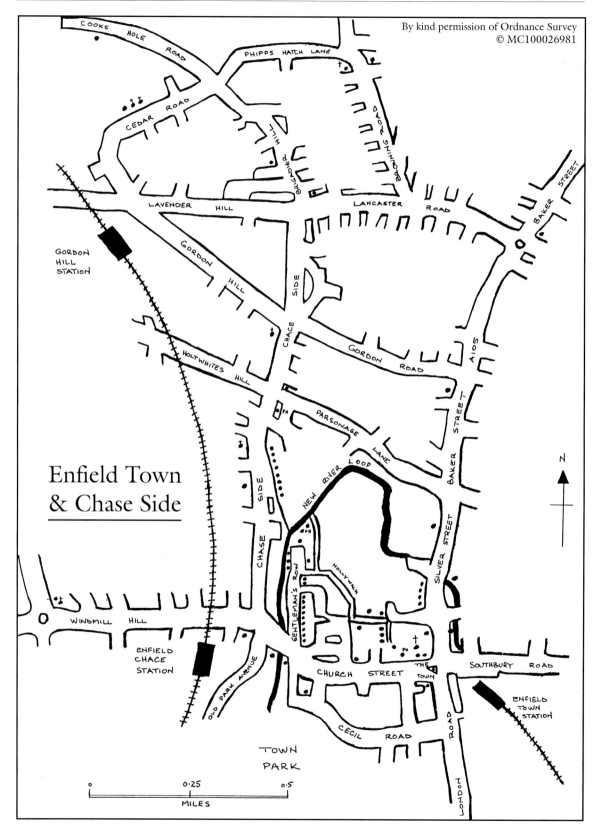

Enfield Town
& Chase Side

Enfield Town, Chase Side & Surrounding Area

Enfield Town manages to retain the feeling of a Tudor market town, despite modern intrusions. Much of the basic street plan was in place by 1572, and many of the listed buildings are grouped around the parish church, grammar school and market place. Unfortunately all that remains of the town green is a large paved traffic island, but the other core features have fared better.

The existing market charter dates from 1618, although the first charter was granted in 1303. After falling into decline in the late C18/early C19 the popular outdoor market now thrives on Thursdays, Fridays and Saturdays.

The Domesday Book of 1086 records a priest, which implies the presence of a church, almost certainly on the site of St Andrew's, the parish church. The earliest part of the present church is C13, though most is of a later date.

The grammar school was founded in 1557, the oldest building next to the church being completed in 1597. Its most celebrated headmaster was Robert Uvedale, a pioneering C17 horticulturalist, who planted and raised a famous cedar of Lebanon in the 'palace' garden close by. Although never a palace, this large manor house with royal associations was demolished in 1927, and is now remembered only by the name of the Palace Gardens shopping precinct built on the site. Wood panelling and a superb stone fireplace and overmantel bearing the Tudor arms have been pre-served in nearby Gentleman's Row.

Just beyond the old town core lay Enfield Chase, a royal hunting ground until its dispersal in 1777. On the edge of this ran the New River, a watercourse built in 1613 by Sir Hugh Myddelton along the 100-foot contour line, from a spring in Ware to Islington, to provide London with fresh water. Although no longer part of the operational watercourse, this tranquil stretch of water with its bird life, old hump-backed bridges and railings, winding its way through Enfield Town to the Town Park, is one of the prime attractions of the Enfield Town Conservation Area. Along part of its length are many fine listed buildings, in particular those in Gentleman's Row.

Charles Lamb and his sister Mary lived in several houses in the immediate vicinity, after their removal from Islington to benefit from the country air. Indeed the area between Chase Side and Baker Street is considered of such historical and architectural significance that it is subject to an Article 4 direction, involving the strictest conservation planning laws applicable, directly under the jurisdiction of the Secretary of State.

For those who associate Enfield with the A10, suburban sprawl and industrial blight, a walk through the Enfield Town Conservation Area can bring nothing but surprise and delight at its many old buildings, quaint alleyways, green spaces and river walkways.

Drinking Fountain, Church Street. 1884, restored 1994. Unlisted.
Survivor of several changes in the road layout, this ornate Victorian drinking fountain, surmounted by two bronze cherubs, stands in the centre of what was Enfield Green in medieval times.

Nos. 3 & 4 The Town. C17. Listed Grade II.
Timber-frame building of two storeys and attic with three flat dormers above the first floor sash windows. Weather-boarded at first-floor level, with a high pitched tiled roof. Despite alterations at ground floor, there have been few external changes since its day as Ebbens Steam Bakery, and it acts as a potent reminder of how the high street looked in times past.

Old Vestry Office, 22 The Town. *c.*1800. Listed Grade II. Small lodge-like hexagonal building in the heart of The Town, nestling unobtrusively between modern shops. A two-storey centre with single-storey side wings canted back, it was once used as the beadle's office with two lock-up cells. Note the round-headed tripartite centre window in round-arched recess.

The C19 wrought iron railings with urn finials and square piers are also listed.

Palace Gardens shopping precinct. Opened 1982. Unlisted.
An interesting roof line, with attention to detail and careful choice of materials, ensures that the shopping centre blends with its surroundings.

Barclays Bank, 20 The Town. 1897. *W. Gilbee Scott.* Listed Local Interest.
Exuberant Flemish Renaissance style, red brick with stone dressings. A pretty cupola rises behind the huge Dutch gable on the frontage.

The world's first cashpoint machine was installed here in 1967.

The King's Head, Market Place, 1899. *Shoebridge & Rising.* Listed Local Interest. Built on the site of an earlier inn, in domestic Old English style. Tile-hung upper storeys, half-timbered gables. Finely detailed doors, carved brackets and etched glass on the ground floor.

Market House, Market Place. 1902. *Sidney M. Cranfield.* Listed Local Interest. Octagonal timber building with classical columns, built to mark the coronation of Edward VII. The style is similar to the ancient Market House which stood here until 1856. It was replaced by a stone Market Cross (now in Myddelton House Garden).

Church of St Andrew, Church Walk. Mainly C14. Listed Grade B.

As so often with old churches this parish church, set back from the bustle of the Market Place, surrounded by trees and old tombstones, is a mixture of building periods. Apart from some C13 masonry in the chancel, the major part, consisting of the nave, north aisle, choir and tower, is late C14 built of random rubble and some flint. The clerestory is early C16 while a restoration in 1824 using red brick added battlements and affected the south aisle and part of the east end.

Inside there is a fine organ case of 1752 and many monuments, including a large brass to Lady Tiptoft (d.1446), a tall monument with reclining figures to Sir Nicholas Raynton (Lord Mayor of London d.1648) and a cartouche to Martha Palmer by Nicholas Stone (1617).

Enfield Grammar School (N. E. Building), Church Walk. Late 16C. Listed Grade II*.

This original part of the school, founded in 1557, is of two storeys and attic with a high pitched tiled roof and three gabled dormers with moulded wood cornices, brick mullions and hood moulds. The main windows are C19 wood-mullioned in stone surrounds. The single lofty ground floor room with its substantial ceiling beams can be seen through the ground floor windows. It is hard to appreciate the fine dimensions of the building owing to a tall screen of trees close by.

Gate detail, Enfield Grammar School

Uvedale House, Church Walk. Early C16. Listed Grade II. Cottage, originally Tudor but much altered externally. It was 're-Tudorized' in the C20, obliterating the simple but pretty brick Georgian façade shown in an old photograph. Two storeys and attic with dormers, painted white brickwork and half-timbering; the square oriel windows on the first floor and wide casements below are modern.

Uvedale Cottage, 1 Holly Walk. C18. Listed Grade II.
Included as part of a group listing with Enfield Grammar School and Uvedale House, this cottage wraps around the northern end of the latter. Two storeys with sash windows and external shutters, white painted brickwork and a high pitched tiled roof, it blends in pleasingly with Uvedale House.

Nos. 13 & 15 Holly Walk.
C19. Listed Local Interest.
Little can be seen of this
secretive pair of cottages except
the fine sash end windows.

Enfield County School, Holly
Walk. 1909. *H. G. Crothall.*
Unlisted.
Pleasing example of MCC
school architecture in brick and
stone, with Art Nouveau domes
in copper on corner turrets
giving an individual touch.
Originally a girls' grammar
school, now the upper school of
a comprehensive. The building
is very similar to the former
Southgate County School in
Fox Lane.

Chapel of Rest, Church Lane. Early C19. Listed Local Interest. This quaint, white-painted building with massive crenellations was built by the Enfield Vestry to house the parish fire engine. The wide arch, which enabled the manual engine to get in and out, was filled in and given a door when the building became a mortuary in 1882. This use continued for some 50 years, after which it was used as offices.

The wrought iron railings and gate into the churchyard came from Fir Tree House, Silver Street, when it was demolished to make way for the Civic Centre.

The Vicarage, Silver Street. Mainly C18. Listed Grade II.

An attractive building when viewed from the churchyard, its two-storey frontage onto the road is curiously blank with few windows. Built in stages from C16-19, the house now forms a square, the main west elevation dating from C18. (North-east corner C16, south and west L-shaped range C18, small north infill section C19). Two storeys plus attic with sash windows, of stock brick with red brick quoins and dressings, the centre breaks forward slightly under the Dutch-style gable.

The late C16 red brick garden wall (east side) with plinth and steep sloped coping is also listed.

Nicon House, 45 Silver Street. 1876. Listed Local Interest. Until 1911 this was the Church of England Girls' School of Industry. The building then housed a boys' preparatory school and, until 1984, the offices and printing works of the *Enfield Gazette*. The pleasant red brick façade with stone dressings has remained more or less unaltered despite the building's many internal changes.

Nos. 58 & 60 Silver Street. Late C18. Listed Grade II.

Listed as a pair, slight alterations over the years have left these two buildings no longer identical. Both are three-storey with sunken basement, of stock brick with stone coped parapet, gauged flat brick arches to sash windows in stucco reveals. No. 58 was altered in mid-C19, changing the ground floor windows to ones with margin lights under segmental gauged brick arches, the central one a blank, round recessed arch with keystone. The single-storey extensions also differ in detail, though both retain the patterned radial fanlight under a round arch.

White Lodge

No. 84 Silver Street

(Opposite, top) **White Lodge,** 68 Silver Street. C17/18. Listed Grade II.

Well known locally as a medical practice, this picturesque building is listed as probably C17 with C18 weatherboarding. Main section is two-storey with a substantial projecting porch, plus attic with tiled roof and dormers, wood modillioned eaves cornice and a delightful triglyph frieze. The casements are late C19 in heavy moulded wood architraves with cornices over. Fine pedimented doorcase with a round-arched fanlight and a cornice and frieze echoing that on the eaves. The right hand part appears older than the main block, with a C19 sash window on the ground floor. Joseph Whitaker, founder of *Whitaker's Almanack*, lived here from 1862 until his death in 1895. It was previously the home of Dr Jacob Vale Asbury, Charles Lamb's doctor.

(Opposite, bottom) **No. 84** Silver Street. Early C19. Listed Grade II.

One-storey three-bay building, built onto a C17 red brick wall which forms most of its front elevation. It was probably an outbuilding to No. 90 with which it is listed for group value. The slate roof is hipped at the left and there is a late C19 two-window right extension with a parapet front.

(Below) **No. 90** Silver Street. Late C18. Listed Grade II.

Directly opposite the uncompromisingly modern Civic Centre, hiding modestly behind trees, this attractive Georgian building is now used by Enfield Council. Two-storey with attic and a sloping mansard roof with three flat dormers, it is yellow brick with a wood modillion cornice and parapet. Six steps bring you to the open pedimented Doric doorcase and plain fanlight set in a moulded architrave.

No. 90 Silver Street

Enfield Civic Centre, Silver Street. 1961 and 1975. *Eric G. Broughton & Assocs.* Unlisted. Twelve-storey tower clad in stainless steel, begun in 1972 to house staff of the newly created London Borough of Enfield, and opened by the Queen Mother in 1975. The original Civic Centre is the long, low brick range of offices and committee rooms to the right. It was opened in 1961, six years after Enfield UDC achieved borough status. In front of the building, the sculpture of the Enfield Beast, emblem of the LBE, is by *R. Bentley Claughton*. In the ornamental gardens, the Enfield Loop of the New River surfaces briefly between culverts.

Enfield Court

Stable Block to Enfield Court

(Opposite, bottom) **Enfield Court,** Silver Street. Late C17/early C18. Listed Grade II.

Once the home of Colonel Sir Alfred Somerset. After the death of his wife, this large, stately building became part of the Grammar School in 1924 and now houses the junior forms. Built in two sections, the seven-window extension is taller and of a later date. Two-storey with attic and basement, yellow brick with red dressings and first floor and cornice stuccoed bands. The high pitched roof of green slate is inset with two curved dormers matching the semi-circular window on the side elevation. The C19 porch has been glazed.

In 1995 the adjacent stable (above) was renovated, with a sympathetic extension, retaining the mounting block in front as a reminder of its origins.

Nos. 172 & 174 Baker Street. C18. Listed Grade II.

An early to mid C18 house of two storeys with attic and dormers set in a tiled gambrel roof, with stone-coped gable ends and parapet and side pilasters. A central round window sits above a cornice hood with a modern reeded door surround. No. 174 comprises the bulk of the house, while No. 172 includes a smaller part and the late C19 shop with weatherboarded side.

(Opposite, bottom) **Brigadier House,** 1 Brigadier Hill. C18. Listed Grade II.

Attractive house standing on a large corner site, aloof from the hustle and bustle of a busy road. Early C18, probably with an earlier core. Two-storey main west front with projecting central bay. Eaves and central pediment have wood modillion cornices. Tiled roof and weatherboarded walls, with late C19 projecting brick ground floor.

The C18 red brick walls round three sides of the garden are also listed, as are the railings and wrought iron gate with overthrow on the west side.

No. 329 Baker Street. C18. Listed Grade II.

End-on to the road, with its south front hidden by creepers and a modern shop on the ground floor, it is easy to miss this potentially charming early to mid C18 red brick house with its Venetian window on the first floor. The gambrel roof has been renewed using machine tiles.

Brigadier House

Nos. 30 & 30A, Brigadier Hill. C18/19. Listed Grade II.

Charming pair of cottages, redolent of a bygone age. Stucco walls with parapet fronts, tiled roofs and identical paint schemes create harmony without hiding individual features. No. 30 St Faith's Cottage (C18) has sash windows with exposed moulded wood frames on the ground floor, and tented canopies at first-floor level. The design of the canopies is echoed by the trellis porch. No. 30A (C19) has a casement window above an early to mid C19 projecting shop front.

(Opposite, top) **St Luke's Church and Parish Room,** Browning Road. 1899. *James Brooks.* Listed Grade C.

Tall, simple red brick church in Early English style with high pitched tiled roofs, shingled turret and stone dressings. Some half-timbering, with herringbone brickwork in gable ends. Tripartite west entrance with blank arcading above. Parish Room in similar style attached to church on south side.

The Cottage, Cooks Hole Lane. C19. Listed Local Interest. (Not illustrated.)

Two storeys, originally with pantiled roof and dormer windows, now with steep pitched thatched roof and eyebrow windows to first floor. Rendered brick walls.

St Luke's Church

Hymus House (formerly St Luke's Vicarage), Browning Road. *c*1900. *James Brooks.* Listed Grade II.
Large, florid, red brick building. Two storeys and attic under massive high pitched hipped roof. Irregular fenestration and numerous quirky Gothic elaborations. Now a nursery school.

Cemetery Chapels & Lodge, Cedar Road.
1870/1. *T. J. Hill*. Listed Grade II.
A group of three cemetery buildings: an Anglican
chapel, a Non-conformist chapel and a lodge, built
for Enfield Burial Board by builder J. & J. Field.
The two mirror-image chapels are matched with
three bays, central porch and two-stage bell tower
with steeple. Decorated Gothic style with offset
buttresses, traceried windows and Welsh slate roof.
Note the details such as the griffin-headed rainwa-
ter downpipes and the decorative iron hinges on
the board doors. The interiors have decorative
stone corbels to the sanctuary arch and supporting
arch-braced roof trusses. The lodge (above) and
gate posts on each side are similar in style.

The pedestrian and carriage gates and the railings are part of the group listing. An unusual
feature is the listed curved metal urinal (right) with
embossed panels and coved top with decorative
bands, attached to the Non-Conformist chapel
(now used as a store) to the right of the porch.

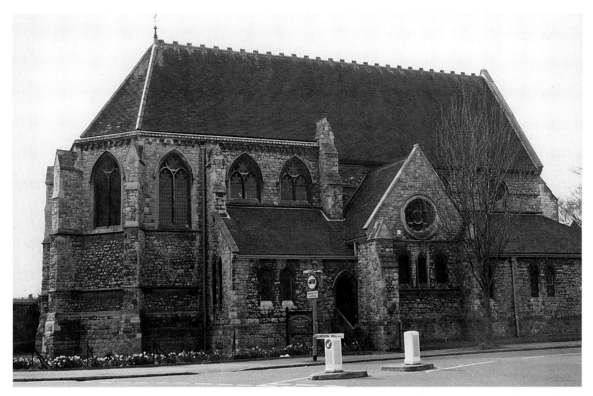

Church of St Michael & All Angels, Chase Side. 1874. *Carpenter & Ingelow.* Listed Grade II.
Square coursed rubble stone with pitched tiled roof. Aisled nave, aisled chancel with tall buttresses and polygonal apse. Clerestory with traceried oculi in semi-circular headed, richly moulded recesses. Its rather squat outward appearance belies a fine interior, including a timber roof of kingpost and arched brace construction.

(Below) **Moon Under Water,** 117 Chase Side. 1838. Unlisted.
Interesting example of a building which has been adapted to many different uses. Built in 1838 as the British Enfield School, which closed in 1901 on the opening of Chase Side School. The building was subsequently used as a public hall, a dairy, a restaurant and is now a pub.

Christ Church, Chase Side 1874. *John Tarring.*
Listed Grade II.
United Reformed church, built for
Congregationalists, in Gothic Revival manner in
coursed squared rubble stone. Slate pitched roofs,
aisled and clerestoried nave and polygonal apse to
chancel. Particularly noteworthy is its elegant, tall
rubble-stoned broach spire, standing on a square
two-stage tower with corner buttresses. Interior
of banded stone; pointed arcade arches on
quatrefoil piers with carved capitals and corbelled
wall shafts. Some Victorian stained glass.

No. 103 Chase Side. C18. Listed Grade II.

Early to mid C18 two-storey house with painted brick front. The stone-coped parapet hides the modern tiles on the high pitched roof. C19 four-panel door in modified entablature surround.

(Below) **Nos 93-99** Chase Side. C17/19. Listed Grade II.

The photograph shows Nos. 93-97. Listed as a group with No. 99 which stands slightly apart. Probably C17 with early to mid C19 frontage of stock brick with stone coped parapet. Nos. 93 & 95 have sunk panels over first-floor windows with gauged brick flat arches and stone cills. No. 97 has an attractive fanlight with interlacing bars matching the ground floor sash window, both under round arches.

Westwood Cottage, 89 Chase Side. Early to mid C19. Listed Grade II.

Two-storey and attic with one gabled dormer in slated roof. Stock brick with stone-coped parapet and gauged round brick arches to the sash windows. A fine doorcase with an open pediment resting on scroll-bracketed cornices, and a moulded architrave around the radial fanlight in a panelled reveal. A bronze plaque reminds passers-by that Charles Lamb lived in this cottage for a short time.

No. 87 Chase Side. C19. Listed Grade II.

Listed for its association with Charles Lamb who lived here from 1827 to 1829, as recorded by the bronze plaque, this house forms part of the group listing of Nos. 77–89. The original attractive C19 front has been sadly desecrated and much altered, including the removal of cornices and the installation of modern casement windows.

No. 85 Chase Side. C18.
Listed Grade II.
Two-storey weatherboarded
cottage, the six-panel door is
now half-glazed under a bracketed flat hood. Box frames have
replaced the sash windows, and
the roof is of modern asbestos
tiles.

(Below) **Nos. 81 & 83** Chase
Side. C19. Listed Grade II.
Possibly once three dwellings,
the central door is no longer
used, with its radial fanlight
blocked in. Yellow brick with
gauged flat brick arches and
stone cills to sash windows.
Gauged round brick arches to
doors. Fairly low pitched
hipped slate roof.

No. 79 Chase Side. C19. Listed Grade II.
This yellow brick early C19 house with later C19 brick parapet hides behind a high laurel hedge. High pitched hipped slated roof and gauged flat brick window arches. Round arch to half-glazed door with patterned fanlight.

(Below) **No. 77** Chase Side. C19. Listed Grade II.
Early to mid C19 two-storey villa of stock brick with parapet. Gauged segmental arch above door, set in a reeded surround with patterned fanlight. The wide wood columned porch is modern.

Gloucester Place Cottages, 22-36 Chase Side. 1823. Listed Grade II. Terrace of eight artisan two-storey cottages of yellow stock brick. Slated hipped roofs, gauged brick flat arches to recessed sash windows, with round arched doorways, some with fanlights.

The Crown and Horseshoes Public House, River View. C19. Listed Grade II.

Early to mid C19 of two storeys, it has a stuccoed front and two half-glazed doors with flat bracketed hoods. Low pitched hipped slated roof with eaves soffit. Set in a quiet position by the New River loop, and with a large garden, this pub was the favoured watering hole of Charles Lamb when he lived in the vicinity.

The four **bridges** over the New River loop, two of which lie close to the pub, are all listed. Early to mid C19, the northernmost one is dated 1841. Of wrought and cast iron, each has a segmental arch with open spandrels, supporting railings, and handrails with scrolled ends.

The Laurels, River View. C17. Listed Grade II.
Timber-framed house re-fronted with stucco and parapet in the early C19 when a back range was added. The central porch with round-headed window is flanked by two-storey square bays. The front garden leads down to the New River loop, access to the house being gained by a small white-painted wooden bridge.

Brecon House, 55 Gentleman's Row. C18. Listed Grade II.

An imposing mid C18 house of three storeys with single storey flanking blocks, each with a Venetian window. The spacious grounds have been the subject of several planning battles over the last 15 years. Yellow brick with red brick dressings, stone cornice and first-floor cill band; the parapet conceals a high pitched, hipped slate roof. The six-panel door is early C19 with a patterned rectangular fanlight set under a console bracketed cornice hood. The three round arched stable doors in the end wall are a particularly attractive feature.

The south garden red brick wall, also mid C18, with sloped coping is also listed. Square piers topped with stone caps and ball finials support an ornamental wrought iron gate with overthrow.

Rivulet House, 32 Gentleman's Row. C19.
Listed Grade II.
Early to mid C19, a compact two-storey brick villa with an attractive Georgian façade, fronting onto a small garden leading down to the New River loop. Well hidden by a thick hedge and surrounded by high walls, this very private house shows only its rear view to passers-by. Under a low pitched hipped slate roof with eaves soffit, the ground-floor windows have red brick arches of herringbone pattern with recessed sash windows and external shutters.

Nos. 27-33 (odd) Gentleman's Row. C19. Listed Grade II.
A row of four early C19 cottages, set in pairs, each with two sash windows and a door set under elliptical gauged brick arches and low pitched hipped slate roofs. A blocked window between each pair maintains the symmetry. Well kept but unpretentious, these cottages are an excellent example of how harmonious a terrace can look when all the original door and window patterns are retained.

The Haven, 16 Gentleman's Row. Early C19. Listed Grade II.

Charming early C19 cottage with painted brick front and rear, external shutters and the original door under a trellis hood. Set well back from the road, with an equally attractive rear leading down to the New River loop, which allowed the occupants dipping rights, the cottage indeed seems a haven from the pressures of modern life.

(Left) **No. 4** Gentleman's Row. Late C18. Listed Local Interest.

One of a picturesque group of four cottages, once called River Cottages, built on an encroachment of land from Enfield Chase. Weatherboarded with casement windows and enclosed porch, its high pitched tiled roof with dormer window makes it stand out from the group.

(Opposite, top) **No. 25** Gentleman's Row. C19. Listed Grade II.

Included for group value with Nos. 1-33 (odd), this mid C19 cottage, originally the stables to its neighbour, served as a corner shop up to the 1960s. Slated roof with eaves soffit and painted brick façade. The door and bow window under the dentilled cornice hood are modern.

No. 4 Gentleman's Row

No 25 Gentleman's Row

(Below) **Archway House,** 23 Gentleman's Row. Mid C18. Listed Grade II.

Built around 1750 this elegant building was the local tavern until just before World War I. As the Archway Tavern it offered an orchard, garden and skittle alley on the long strip of land to its rear which now forms Holly Walk. The ground-floor left window is set in a round-arched recess with stuccoed impost blocks to match the arched carriageway, from which the house derives its name, leading to Chapel Street (formerly Love's Row). The brick dentilled cornice and parapet with projecting central bay and the pillared doorcase with its original fanlight enhance the pleasing proportions.

Archway House

Sedgecope

Eastbury

Sedgecope, 21 Gentleman's Row. C17 Listed Grade II.

A C17 timber-framed house with an early C18 dark red brick front and high pitched roof with two dormers. The fine doorcase of fluted pilasters and entablature is particularly notable set directly opposite a well-screened small garden, originally an encroachment on Enfield Chase. All the houses down this part of Gentleman's Row have similar encroachments, separated from the houses by the footpath. These plots were sold to the occupants in 1777 when Enfield Chase, originally the monarch's private hunting ground, was sold off by the parish.

(Left, bottom) **Eastbury,** 19 Gentleman's Row. C17. Listed Grade II.

Similar to its neighbour to the north, this C17 timber-framed house had a new façade in the early C18 with red brick, and also boasts a good doorcase with fluted pilasters and entablature. The high pitched tiled roof with cornice and stone-coped parapet has three flat dormers. During an extensive restoration in 1950 hay was found under the roof tiles, an ancient form of insulation. At the end of the garden a single-storey building, now a garage, once housed a small Dame school; the house was then known as the School House.

(Opposite, top) **Clarendon Cottage,**
17 Gentleman's Row. C16. Listed Grade II*.

Originally a C16 timber-framed hall house of two bays, an extension was added in the C17 when the whole was refronted and covered in painted stucco. The sash windows, those on the ground floor with external shutters, are C18, but the bull's-eye window is a modern addition. The door of six fielded panels, now top-glazed, sits in a raised stucco surround with Gothic raised border and break-front doorcase. A picturesque cottage much favoured by local artists, a wooden plaque notes its association with Charles and Mary Lamb who stayed for some months on two occasions (1825 and 1827) when it was a boarding house.

Clarendon Cottage

(Right) **Fortescue Villas,** 13 & 15 Gentleman's Row. mid C19. Listed Grade II.

Built in the 1840s on the site of an ancient large timber-framed house (probably C15) called Fortescue Hall (demolished 1813), from which they derive their name, these two large houses have been divided horizontally into four spacious flats. At the turn of the last century they housed a school before becoming a children's home. Strong featured, with bracketed eaves and a slate roof set above sash windows with cambered heads, keystones and slatted external shutters. There are canted bays of brick at ground and basement level.

The C19 cast iron railings with ball and spike finials are also listed.

The Coach House, Gentleman's Row. C16. Listed Grade II. Unusual L-shaped timber-frame building of upper-cruck construction, originally a barn. It was upgraded to the coach house and stables for Fortescue Hall, and on the latter's demolition in 1813, for Fortescue Lodge. With a high pitched roof and mainly weatherboarded, it was sympathetically converted to a house in the 1950s, incorporating a modern oriel window in the gable end and small casement windows elsewhere.

Fortescue Lodge, 11 Gentleman's Row. C17. Listed Grade II. Originally the stableman's cottage for Fortescue Hall, this late C17 timber-framed building was converted to a sizeable house in 1710 and given a new façade in early Georgian style, covered with white stucco. The term 'Lodge' was a Victorian embellishment, no doubt to evoke memories of the days when Enfield Chase was the royal hunting ground – before this it was called Fortescue House. The sash windows have blind cases and the fluted doorcase is early C19.

The sweeping bow of early C19 cast iron railings with spearhead finials is also listed.

Elm House, Nos. 7 & 9 Gentleman's Row. C17. Listed Grade II.

An C18 brick parapet front disguises an earlier house, probably C17. The six-panel door has a rectangular fanlight with interlaced bars while the sash windows are set in gauged flat brick arches. Now divided into flats, the southern extension, originally part of Elm House, has been split off to form No. 7 with modern additions. The house has served as a school, a Girl Guide hall, a store for antique furniture once visited by Queen Mary, and a convalescent home for wounded soldiers in World War I.

The fine C18 wrought iron railings with side piers and ornamental overthrow, set on a modern low brick wall, are also listed.

Little Park, 5 Gentleman's Row. C17/20.
Listed Grade II.

Although ostensibly a typical large Edwardian house, Little Park has been substantially altered, with parts dating back to Tudor times. Before its Edwardian transformation it had a rather ugly Georgian façade. Its most notable feature is the single-storey extension known as the Tudor Room, built to house a superb stone fireplace bearing the royal arms, the crowned Tudor Rose, the crowned portcullis and the initials 'E. R.'. There is some fine panelling also with the royal arms and the inscription in Latin: *The favour of the King is like dew upon the grass.* These magnificent pieces were removed from the nearby Enfield Palace, an old manor house, on its demolition in 1927. A weathervane, taken from the palace of Theobalds, is another reminder of Enfield's royal associations.

(Opposite, bottom) **Post Office,** 27 Church Street. 1906. Listed Local Interest.

Elegant stone-clad ground floor in Free Classical style. Moulded sash window surrounds with attached Ionic columns. Royal arms in carved brick on pediment.

Note the group of K6 telephone kiosks (not illustrated) at the side of the building, in Little Park Gardens.

The Public Offices

Post Office

(Above) **The Public Offices,**
1 Gentleman's Row. C18. Listed Grade II.

A large central block of three storeys and two-storey side wings, this imposing Georgian building was once a magnificent private house with a large garden and lake to the rear. Bought in 1888 by the Enfield Board of Health it has served many purposes including the district's first public library. It is currently the Registry Office. Built of stock brick with parapet fronts, the centre one having a modillioned cornice, pediment and round window, there is a fine sash window on the first floor in a stuccoed entablature surround with pediment over a balustrade below, offsetting the equally fine Ionic doorcase. An unfortunate C19 square bay of three-storey height covers the right-hand windows of the centre section, marring the building's excellent proportions.

The red brick C18 wall to the north forecourt, with flat buttresses and a stone-capped square end pier of yellow brick with ball finial, is also listed.

Central Library, Cecil Road. 1912. Unlisted.
Reassuring though slightly pretentious two-storey building in red brick with stone quoins, segmental pediment in central bay, festooned circular window, and Ionic doorway with broken pediment. The Library Green, extending to Church Street, is classified as metropolitan open land.

River House, 90 Church Street. C18. Listed Local Interest.
Three-bay, three-storey C18 house with C19 bay windows.

(Opposite, bottom) **Magistrates Court,** Windmill Hill. 1900. *H. T. Wakelam*. Unlisted.
Substantial single-storey building, red brick with ornate stone dressings and central gable.

(Above) **Data Connection,** 100 Church Street. 1987. Unlisted. Lively office complex alongside the New River Loop, in dark brick with stone-faced floor bands and tinted windows.

Magistrates Court

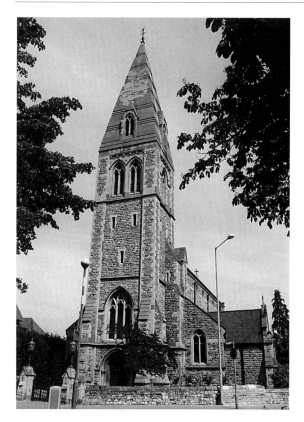

St Mary Magdalene, The Ridgeway (jct. Windmill Hill). 1883.
William Butterfield. Listed Grade B.
Walls are of coursed rubble with ashlar facings and dressed quoins. The tiled roofs, hipped and ridged, rise to an imposing steeple with bell chamber. Handsome chancel with coloured marbles and tiles, roof and wall paintings.

Ridge End, The Ridgeway. 1883.
William Butterfield. Listed Grade II.
Formerly the Vicarage, this irregular building was designed to match the church, with polygonal bay and oriel. Chequerwork of dressed stone alternating with rubble in gables of porch and west end. Listed as a group with the church and forecourt walls.

Bush Hill Park & Winchmore Hill

Bush Hill Park, which includes some of the oldest suburban developments in Enfield, contains the remains of the earliest known settlement in the district. Numerous Roman finds were crowned by evidence of a Roman settlement between Lincoln Road and Main Avenue following excavations (prior to redevelopment) in 1974-6.

After the Roman occupation the area remained rural until the early 1870s when the large country estate belonging to Bush Hill Park, a mansion on the slope of the hill, was sold and broken up for housing. The first houses in Wellington Road and Village Road were offered for sale in 1878. Five years later *The British Architect* featured 'Country Homes in Bush Hill Park' in Queen Anne's Place and Dryden Road. These substantial detached or semi-detached houses in spacious, tree-lined roads, were in great demand, especially after Bush Hill Park Station opened in 1880. At the corner of Dryden Road an ornate, substantial building

(*c*1900) with corner turret, was formerly a bank, built to serve the prosperous middle-class residents of the new suburb.

Many of the well-designed buildings have been replaced by flats or modern town houses, others have been converted into retirement homes for elderly residents who appreciate the peaceful charm of the area. In an attempt to prevent the wholesale redevelopment that overtook the Victorian villas on the Bycullah estate in the 1960s, Dryden Road and neighbouring streets were designated as a conservation area in 1987.

Soon after the Great Eastern Railway opened Bush Hill Park Station, terraces of small, working-class houses sprang up east of the line, many of them occupied by railway employees (First Avenue was begun in 1880). Development continued until, by the mid Thirties, only a few pockets of land remained vacant. The last sizeable development was the New River estate, including Sittingbourne Avenue and Faversham Avenue.

Clarendon Arch and Tunnel,
Bush Hill, N21. Listed Grade II. The arch ring of Portland stone bears a fine shield of arms with mantling helm and the crest of Myddelton, and the inscription: 'This arch is at the end of a long, barrel-vaulted brick tunnel which carries the Salmons Brook beneath the New River'. Above the northwest side of the tunnel is a stone with the inscription: 'This bank of earth was raised and formed to support the Channel of the New River. And the frame of timber and lead which served that purpose 173 years was removed and taken away. MDCCLXXXVI Peter Holford Esquire, Governor'.

English Heritage included

Clarendon Arch and Tunnel on the national Buildings at Risk list in 1998 and 1999/2000, describing its condition as 'poor'. In March 2000 Thames Water, the owners, announced a proposed refurbishment programme with the construction of a public viewing platform.

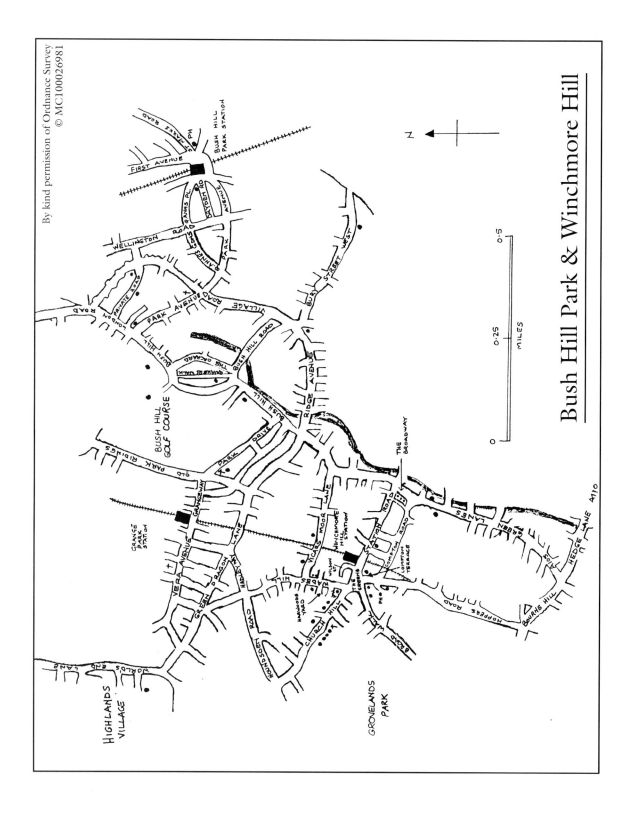

By kind permission of Ordnance Survey
© MC100026981

Bush Hill Park & Winchmore Hill

Bush Hill Park Golf Club, Carr's Lane. C17 with additions. Listed Local Interest.

Built in the early C17 as the mansion of Old Park, the house was added to in the C19. Further additions and alterations, including the installation of obtrusive picture windows, were made in the C20 when it became the club house. The golf club moved to Old Park in 1913 and took over the mansion ten years later when their old club house was burnt down. The mansion, which once belonged to the C19 antiquarian Edward Ford, is surrounded by a circular earthwork, the remains of an Iron Age hill fort. Old Park is the 'old park' mentioned in the Domesday Book of 1086.

The stable buildings (below) south-west of the house are also listed.

The Tower, Quakers Walk, N21. C19. *North London Estates Co.* Listed Grade II.

The 40ft folly tower was built on a site formerly occupied by substantial houses erected for the Quakers who attended the nearby Meeting House. It was to be part of the works to provide an improved water supply to houses on the newly-built estate. The Tower is square, in yellow brick with dressings of red brick and stone, with a projecting round staircase turret on the south side. Some windows are arrow slits, others lancets with gauged brick pointed or flat arches, with a large modern louvred window to the top stage.

The works were sold to the New River Company and the tower was never used for its original purpose. The ground floor was converted into accommodation for a company employee. Further floors were converted by the present owners.

Bush Hill Sluice, Bush Hill Road. Late C18. *Robert Mylne.* Listed Grade II.

Built for the New River Company as part of the works of the New River, which was engineered in 1613 by Sir Hugh Myddelton to bring a purer water supply to London. Gates were operated from the sluice house to control the flow of water over the Bush Hill frame (see Clarendon Arch).

Library and Clinic, Ridge Avenue/Church Street. 1963 *Brian van Breda.* Unlisted.
Striking monopitch roofs, broad gables and floor-to-eaves windows invigorate this distinguished L-shaped building, Designed in the Edmonton Borough Architect's Department, it makes the most of a corner site.

Salisbury House, Bury Street West, N9.
Late C16/early C17. Listed Grade II*.
This timber-framed house, plastered with red tiled roofs, is the oldest building in the area, a relic of the ancient hamlet of Bury Street. Upper storeys oversail the first and second-floor levels on all sides. The west front, of three gables, has a semi-octagonal gabled turret cutting into central and southern gables. Some C19 and modern casements and a C18 or early C19 oriel bay with Gothic glazing bars and some sashes with glazing bars · *c*1800.

The history of the house is uncertain: it may have been part of a much larger building. The name could have come from the Cecil family (the Marquess of Salisbury owned land in Edmonton) or from an estate known as Sayesbury. There is evidence of a priest hole in the basement with a false chimney to provide ventilation.

First floor includes a room with C17 panelling and fireplace, sold to an Edinburgh museum in 1907 but now reinstalled. The fireplace reveals contain fragments of C17 paintings.

Before being acquired by Edmonton Urban District Council in 1936 the house was a private residence, a school, and then a private residence again. It had a year-long restoration 1992 and is now leased to a local arts organisation.

Walls (probably C17) east of the house and south-west of the garden are also listed.

Nursery School, Dryden Road. *c*1900. Unlisted. Handsome, nicely-detailed former bank with pillared porch. Curved hoods on the dormer windows echo the domed corner turret.

(Below) **Bush Hill Park Hotel,** St Mark's Road. Late C19. Unlisted.
Typical railway hotel, dominating the approach to Bush Hill Park Station. Glorious mish-mash of styles, embellished by gables, dormer windows, verandah and corner bow topped by a domed roof.

The Anchorage, 13 Village Road. Late C19, *Thomas Tayler Smith.* Listed Grade II.
On the corner of Private Road and Village Road (the original address was 12 Private Road) this is one of two houses built in Private Road in the Arts & Crafts style and described in *The British Architect* in 1883 as 'bijou houses'. Comments included: 'one of the most satisfactory examples of hipped roofs which can been seen in the park' and 'perhaps the most perfect application of electric lighting to domestic purposes which has yet been developed'.

The other 'bijou house' was the picturesque, half-timbered Halcyon (demolished 1968) built in 1874 by the local architect *A. H. Mackmurdo* for his mother.

Brooklyn, 8 Private Road. C19. *A. H. Mackmurdo.* Listed Grade II
Built in 1887 by *Arthur Heygate Mackmurdo* for his brother, next-door to, but in a very different style from, Halcyon. The severe shape and flat roof were considered daringly original and aroused considerable interest. The walls are pebble-dashed, with moulded strings at first-floor cill and lintel levels, with a moulded cornice and parapet with ball finials above. Terracotta figurines cap the four pillars which support the roof; the ground-floor window surrounds are terracotta reliefs of fruit and flowers. Little original work remains inside apart from a screen of three shallow elliptical arches in the hall.

Denbydene/Castleleigh, London Road. Late C19. Listed Local Interest. Designed as a poor man's romantic castle, with bricks selected to give the impression of castle stonework. Mrs Denby, the first occupier, named it Denbydene, but the house is now called Castleleigh and is divided into two separate dwellings.

No. 65 London Road. C19. Listed Local Interest. Two-storey, brick-built Victorian villa with imposing entrance and nicely-detailed windows, typical of the substantial houses that once lined London Road.

Winchmore Hill

Once the heart of an isolated woodland hamlet, Winchmore Hill Green had become the centre of a well-established village by the end of the C17 with houses radiating out along Church Hill (then called Winchmore Hill Lane), Wades Hill (Middle Chase Lane), Station Road (Middle Lane), Vicars Moor Lane and Hoppers Road. A Quaker community had been active since 1688 although the present Friends Meeting House in Church Hill was not built until 1790.

The village remained virtually unchanged until well into the C19. Until 1871, when the Great Northern Railway opened a station at Winchmore Hill, villagers relied on a horse bus to transport them to Edmonton or further afield. An electric tram service along Green Lanes, which began in 1907, stimulated a shopping parade at The Broadway to cater for the fast-growing suburb.

Between 1900 and 1914 much of the area became covered by semi-detached villas, many in red brick offset by white-painted stonework and woodwork. They were characterised by impressive front entrances featuring doors richly decorated with Art Nouveau-pattern glass, elaborate wooden porches and tiled garden paths.

The opening of Grange Park Station in 1910 gave rise to an estate of well-built, finely-detailed houses, designed in the Arts & Crafts idiom by *Richard Metherell*. The area at the top of The Chine, where a series of large, detached houses sweep around the curve of the road, sums up a development which some regard as representing one of the high points of English domestic architecture.

Between the wars, Winchmore Hill became almost completely covered by houses, mostly semi-detached but with individual touches like the mock-Tudor, garden-city-like Broadfields Estate. Substantial detached houses appeared in Eversley Crescent, outclassed only by those in Broad Walk, known locally as Millionaires' Row. This spacious road, lined with mature oak trees and exclusive red brick herringbone pavements, contains examples of inter-war styles ranging from Arts & Crafts and Mock Tudor to the much rarer Hollywood Moderne (*Blue Firs,* No. 68, dated 1935).

Since 1945 building has been restricted to infill development, except for the massive housing estate on the Highlands Hospital site.

The King's Head, The Green. 1899. Unlisted. (Not illustrated.)
Typically flamboyant Victorian 'Railway Hotel', dominant feature of The Green and its finest building, Three storeys in red brick with stone dressings, steeply pitched gabled roof. Striking corner turret with steeply-spired roof marks junction of The Green with Wades Hill and Church Hill. The space behind the twin arched stable entrances on the Church Hill side originally housed the village fire engine.

Rowantree House/Woodside House, The Green. Early C18. Listed Grade II.

Originally a single property. **Rowantree House** comprises five bays and three storeys, the third being an attic under a slate mansard roof with three dormers. Façade of white-painted brick with dentilled cornice below parapet. Half of **Woodside House** lies under a continuation of the roof of Rowantree House with the other half (an apparently later extension) under a flat roof hidden behind the parapet. Though of considerable frontage the houses have little depth.

K6 Telephone Kiosk, The Green. 1935. *Sir Giles Gilbert Scott.* Listed Grade II. (Not illustrated.)
Thanks to a campaign led by the Thirties Society, selected K6 telephone kiosks in conservation areas, and their rare 1927 predecessors, K2, were spared from British Telecom's modernisation plans in 1985.

Repton Court, 23 The Green. 1998/9. *Stephens Design Associates.* Unlisted. (Not illustrated.)
This key corner site on The Green was previously disfigured by a row of garages, the burnt-out shell of an auction room, a car park and a 1960s car showroom. Before 1965 it was occupied by a terrace of C18 shops and cottages built tight to the pavement. Repton Court is a block of flats with frontages to The Green and Hoppers Road, its large mass broken up by creating the impression of individual properties in a terrace. This is particularly effective with the two reproduction Georgian houses on the important Green frontage. Though commercial viability has determined the evident height and bulk of the building, this is compensated by the thoughtful design and use of traditional materials. The development has given some weight to this important corner of The Green and provides a visual balance to offset the façade of tall buildings on its north side.

Rowantree House and Woodside House

The Old Bakery, 212 Hoppers Road. Late C17/ early C18. Listed Grade II.

A remnant of the pre-Victorian village, this timber-framed building is one of the most important visual reference points on The Green, its low, white-washed gable-end an obvious reminder of Winchmore Hill's past identity. All the evidence points towards its original use as a farmhouse which had an oven installed *c*1815 for baking bread and at the same time had a shop-front fitted. Part of the fabric is probably considerably older.

In the early and mid C19 it was part of a farm property with fields extending down the hill to Green Lanes. It had a sizeable garden to the front facing The Green and a farmyard to the rear with a large barn and an entrance near the junction with Compton Road. In the 1880s John Butson, a local speculative builder, acquired both, building shops (Nos. 17-21 The Green) in the front garden and a row of cottages (Compton Terrace) on the former farmyard. The building continued as a bakery and shop until the 1960s, after which it became an antique shop, then the residence it is today. The original ovens remain as does the early C19 shop front with its fluted wooden columns.

Compton Terrace, Hoppers Road. 1880s. Unlisted. (Not illustrated.)
Wilson Street. 1880-90. Unlisted.
Built in the late C19 to meet the demand for small workers' cottages in the village. Architecturally un-exceptional, but a minor delight in this setting. Note the attractive wrought iron porch brackets on some of the cottages in the northern, red brick section of Wilson Street.

The Salisbury Arms, Hoppers Road. 1935. Un-listed. (Not illustrated.)
An underrated and undervalued building, this Jacobethan-style pub is modest in demeanour and strangely missable at first glance. Closer inspection reveals an interesting building with acceptably convincing retrospective styling in red brick, with stone mullions to leaded casement windows, under a low roofline with hipped dormers and stepped gables.

The Old Bakery

Devon House, Church Hill. C18, rebuilt 1985 *Charles Leekham Associates.* Listed Grade II. Typically rural-Georgian brick house, largely rebuilt in 1985 as a replica of an identically proportioned though more humble predecessor. The careful use of traditional materials is a reassuring example of what can be achieved with new buildings in conservation areas. Note the three-bay wing to the side of the main building, with its twin stone arches under the first floor leading to an attractive triangular courtyard; also at the rear the idiosyncratic modern touch of a curved glass wall and ceiling sheltering the first-floor stair landing.

FRIENDS
MEETING
HOUSE

Friends' Meeting House

St Paul's Church, Church Hill. 1828, chancel 1889. *John Davies.* Listed Grade C.

Built as a practical church at modest expense to serve a growing population previously obliged to walk to Southgate or Edmonton for worship. Designed in a style known as 'Churchwarden's Gothic' at a time of economic depression following the Napoleonic Wars. Perpendicular Gothic, yellow stock brick relieved by some attractive stone dressings, particularly the impressive frontispiece and bell turret above the west entrance. The 1889 addition of a chancel transformed the warehouse-like interior into a convincing, colourful church. Best bits include huge chancel arch, wooden chancel ceiling in the manner of an upturned boat, stained glass windows, font in coloured Devonshire marble, and carved stone reredos depicting Leonardo Da Vinci's 'Last Supper'.

St Paul's Vicarage, Church Hill. 1913. Unlisted. (Not illustrated)

Large, rambling, old-style country rectory. A tall boundary wall partly obscures the unimpressive front but the back is a good example of Queen Anne Revival in red brick under a tiled roof with an abundance of hips, valleys and tall chimney stacks.

(Opposite, bottom) **Friends' Meeting House,** Church Hill. 1688, rebuilt 1790. **Caretaker's cottage** 1911. Listed Grade II.

Charming combination of Georgian aesthetic sensibility and plain, simple Quaker values. Unpretentious but nicely-proportioned single storey yellow brick building with a pediment over the road front, and underneath this a bracketed cornice hood sheltering a central double door flanked by large sash windows with delicate glazing bars, shutters and gauged brick arches. Sits in peaceful grounds of about one acre, effectively preserving the original village atmosphere and setting. Note quaint little caretaker's cottage and boundary walls (late C18/early C19) which are curved at front, originally to provide a turning circle for carriages in this once narrow country lane.

Stone Hall Lodge, Church Hill. Mid-C19. Listed Local Interest.

White-painted brick Victorian cottage which served as the lodge to nearby Stone Hall (from 1872 until its demolition in 1932) but, as evidenced by its appearance on the 1867 Ordnance Survey map, predated it by several years. Wooden bargeboards, simple glazing-bar pattern on the ground floor front bay, cosy verandah to the side. External appearance spoilt by a satellite dish.

(Above and opposite, top) **Woodside Cottages,** Church Hill. Late C18/early C19. Listed Grade II (Group Value).

Three picturesque weatherboarded cottages form a highly effective group on a leafy hill against a backdrop of woodland. They present a charming rural scene, surprisingly little changed since Winchmore Hill was a village in the Middlesex countryside. Until these cottages were listed, only good luck protected them from the threat of demolition to widen this narrow stretch of road.

Woodstock, No. 1; stock brick with boarded front, attractive wooden verandah with tented lead roof, bracketed eaves soffit. **The Old School House,** *c*1780 once served as the village school. (note wooden trellis porch with gable) **The Cottage** originally had wooden sashes; the leaded casements are modern additions.

The Cottage, Woodside Cottages

Nos. 17-21 (odd) Wades Hill. Early/mid C19. Listed Grade II (Group Value).
Row of three two-storey brick cottages with sash windows under shallow, hipped slate roofs. York stone paving to fronts. The largest, No. 17, is double-fronted with a reproduction pedimented doorcase, and has a small coach-house to the side.

Nos. 23-29 (odd) Wades Hill Early/mid C19. Listed Grade II (Group Value).

Group of weatherboarded vernacular cottages with simple but appealing bracketed door hoods. Though now gentrified, the cottages have survived almost intact save the addition of modern but arguably sympathetic oriel bows on the ground floors of **Nos. 22 and 29** and the provision of off-street parking on the former front gardens. Until the early 1990s **No.23** still had its earth ground floor.

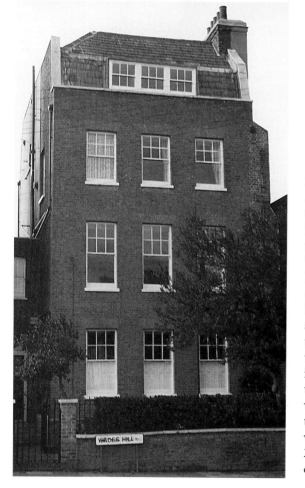

Harwood's Yard, off Wades Hill. Mid C19. Unlisted. (Not illustrated)

Small Victorian estate cottages, charming but architecturally unexceptional, set behind attractive front gardens in a quiet, secluded close where echoes of Winchmore Hill's rural past still linger.

(Left) **Glenwood House,** 28 Wades Hill. C18. Listed Grade II.

All the literature on Winchmore Hill labels this tall Georgian stock brick house as one of a former pair, but this assumption is open to doubt. An early C18 three-storey red brick Queen Anne-style house, The Elms, stood next door before its demolition in 1935 to make way for Keble School. Cartographical evidence suggests that at the beginning of C19 both house constituted a single property with a stable block to the south and extensive garden to the rear. By the mid C19 maps show it divided into two properties, Glenwood (newly 'modernised' with its present yellow brick façade) being the Vicarage to St Paul's Church with The Elms as a church-warden's residence. Both houses were extended at the rear in the late C19. Glenwood lost its side wing when the neighbouring terrace of Nos. 16-26 was built *c*1898-1901, with only the entrance door and window above it remaining.

Nos. 74-76 Vicars Moor Lane, and door detail of No. 76

Nos. 66-76 (even) Vicars Moor Lane.
1870s. Listed Grade II (Group Value).
The elegant classical proportions and styling of these villas suggest a date *c*1800, but they are contemporary with the opening of the railway line in the 1870s. However, **No. 70** has evidence of *c*1840 work within, which suggests a rebuild and enlargement of older property. **Nos. 70-76** form an attractive terrace in stock brick with large sash windows (note the delectably thin glazing bars) and heavy, solid prostyle Tuscan porches with dentil cornicing to front doors. **No. 66-68A** is a detached double-fronted house in the same style now divided into four properties.

Nos. 82-108 (even) Vicars Moor Lane. Some Listed Local Interest.

Rare and well-preserved stretch of C19 village street with examples from early, mid and late C19. Together with Nos. 66-76, this group forms a separate conservation area. Because of this planning status it has been thought sufficient to list only **Nos. 82, 84, 100-106** as being of local interest. **No. 108,** formerly a chapel, was built in 1883 and used until 1982 by the Strict Baptists. Now carefully converted into an interesting residence, the large tripartite gothic-arch window above the entrance door gives a glimpse of the balustraded staircase giving access to the installed first floor.

(Top) **Nos. 104-106 Vicars Moor Lane.**
(Left) **No. 100 Vicars Moor Lane.**

Sorting Office, Station Road. 1904.
Listed Grade II.
Small two-storey baroque building of red brick with stone dressings. Three-bay front with slightly canted outer bays, the whole treated as one large Dutch gable. Royal Arms of Edward VII at ground floor centre. Entrance, on the right return, is under a round arch, with moulded architrave and keystone, framed in entablature surround with swags in the spandrels.

The **ornamental wrought iron railings** are also Listed Grade II.

Police Station,
687 Green Lanes. 1915. *J. D. Butler*. Listed Grade II. This red brick Edwardian police station with its curved gables and ground-floor bow window has all the stout appearance of a constable's helmet. The attractive wrought iron holder for the blue lamp at the entrance provides a traditional finishing touch. A reminder of an era of policing which has all but disappeared.

Cedar House

Former Ambulance Station

Shops, Winchmore Hill Broadway, Green Lanes. 1904-11. *James Edmondson.* Unlisted. (Not illustrated) Opulent in their day, these parades now represent the crusty edges of Edwardian Winchmore Hill and add a welcome touch of exuberance to this otherwise architecturally arid stretch of main road. Best bits are **No. 790** with its pedimented Dutch gable and spired cupola and **Nos. 715-727** which sweep round in a curve from Compton Road. There is a strong similarity to Edmondson's work at Muswell Hill Broadway.

(Opposite, top) **Cedar House,** 698 Green Lanes. Mid C19. Listed Local Interest. This stuccoed Victorian Italianate country villa, with grounds backing onto the New River, dates from a time when Green Lanes lived up to its name. Formerly a residence, now converted into a nursery school, most of the original exterior features remain intact. Note the charming laced iron verandah with tented lead roof to the south side.

Grange Park Methodist Church, Old Park Ridings. 1938 *C. H. Brightiff.* Unlisted.
Popularly known as the Church in the Orchard, this handsome Art Deco building makes the most of a prominent corner site. Brick-built with square tower and buttresses, rectangular windows and stone carvings above the doorways. The church halls were added in 1970.

(Opposite, bottom) **Former Ambulance Station,** Highlands Hospital, World's End Lane. 1884-7. *Pennington and Brigden.* Listed Grade II.
Now incorporated into a 1990s residential development, this was the Ambulance Station to the former Northern Fever Hospital, re-named Highlands Hospital in 1948. The symmetrical building of red and yellow brick has a central opening for the carriage which conveyed the infectious patients to the hospital. There is an iron shelter of three bays at the rear.

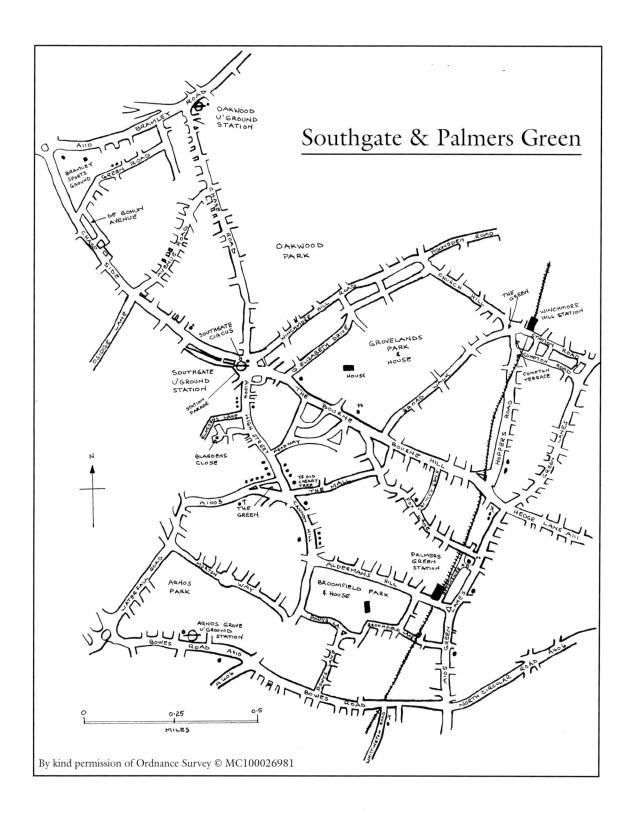

Southgate & Palmers Green

Southgate & Palmers Green

Originally in the parish of Edmonton, Southgate developed from a settlement which grew up round the south gate to Enfield Chase. The gate stood roughly at today's junction of Winchmore Hill Road and Chase Road, in an area then covered by dense woodland. Another hamlet, South Street, clustered around Southgate Green. It was several centuries before the two settlements became linked by Southgate High Street.

The area remained surprisingly rural until the 1920s, partly because of poor transport links but also thanks to the intransigence of landowners like the Taylors of Grovelands and the Walkers of Arnos Grove who refused to break up their estates for development. Land from these estates later formed Grovelands Park (where some of the ancient woodland survives) and Arnos Park.

A few streets, including Chelmsford Road, Reservoir Road, Avenue Road, and Nursery Road, were laid out in the early 1850s, when Southgate's main link to the wider world was a horse bus to the nearest railway station: Colney Hatch, until Palmers Green station was opened in 1871. Development began in earnest after the London General Omnibus Company extended its route to Southgate Green and reached a frenzy when the Piccadilly Line was extended to Arnos Grove in 1932 and to Southgate, Oakwood and Cockfosters the following year.

Thanks to green belt planning restrictions, development since the Second World War has been confined mainly to infilling and the blocks of flats which have replaced older houses, notably in Chase Side, Chase Road and Avenue Road.

Oakwood Station, Bramley Road. 1932.
C. H. James and Charles Holden. Listed Grade II. Originally called Enfield West Station, re-named Oakwood in 1946.
Symmetrically planned building of multi-coloured stock brick walls with reinforced-concrete roof and ring beams with high rectangular ticket hall. Flat roof with projecting eaves and plain concrete band below. Metal windows with horizontal oblong panes, a feature of all Holden stations on the Piccadilly Line.

Station sign with pedestrian shelter at the base is also listed Grade II.

Chicken Shed Theatre, Chase Side, Southgate N14, *RHWL Partnership,* Unlisted.
Constructed in 1994/5 this building provides a permanent home for a community theatre company's pioneering work with young disabled people and their able-bodied peers.

(Below) **De Bohun School**, Green Road, 1936 *W. T. Curtis and H. W. Burchett,* MCC Architects Department. Listed Grade II.
One of the most modern buildings in the borough to be listed (1994). The compact school, with the adjacent library and health centre are an English interpretation of Continental style of the time and are of high quality architectural design. The buildings are named after the De Bohun family who owned the land in the middle of the C12.

Clock Tower, Bramley Road Sports Ground. 1930s. Unlisted.

De Bohun Library, Health Centre and Gates, Green Road. 1938-9 *W. T. Curtis and H. W. Burchett* MCC Architects Department. Listed Grade II. The health centre and library, a neat cubic composition, was built with red diaper brick to complement the larger De Bohun School, with which it forms a group. The metal casement windows generally have horizontal panes, whilst those to ground floor and stairtower are arranged in vertical strips. Those on first floor form a continuous horizontal band under a moulded deep eaves cornice. The front gates are in the art deco style. The library has now been closed.

Church of St Andrew, Chase Side. 1903. *A. R. Barker. Extensions 1916 by Barker & Kirk.* Listed Grade C.
Built to the design of local architect A. R. Barker, the sanctuary and north chancel aisle were added in 1916. Of particular interest are the flying buttresses to the clerestory. Inside, a wide nave with passage aisles, the three bays continuing without break through two more bays screening the transepts. Modified perpendicular style windows, the west window of great size. Stone piers, red brick dressings, yellow brick walls. Projecting, pent, one-storey west baptistery with central canted bay.

Southgate Station. 1932/3. *Charles Holden.*
Listed Grade II
Constructed in multi-coloured stock brick with tiled internal wall surfaces. Reinforced concrete tiered flat roofs with projected eaves. Central pagoda-like lantern with bronze finial. The low circular booking-hall roof with continuous clerestory windows is carried on a central column around which was the original booking office. There are original bronze windows in the integrated shopping arcade and around the building.

Southgate Station Parade, 1932. *Charles Holden.*
Listed Grade II.
Two-storey curved parade designed to complement the station building, with shops recessed behind mosaic-clad pillars to the ground floor and with full-height bows to each end. The bronze window frames and glazing pattern are original as is the clock in the centre of the upper storey. These buildings are listed as an integral part of the station complex along with the two reinforced concrete station signs surrounded by seats, at each end of the concourse around the station building.

Grovelands Priory Hospital, (original block only). The Bourne. 1797. *John Nash*. Listed Grade I.

One of only two Grade I listed buildings in the borough, Grovelands House has been described as the finest Neoclassical villa of its kind in the London area. Built as Southgate Grove for Walker Gray, a brandy merchant, it was designed by John Nash in partnership with Humphry Repton, who laid out the grounds. At the time Nash was making a comeback after bankruptcy, but although his most famous buildings were yet to come, this elegant, finely detailed house contains innovations and surprises.

Four impressive Ionic order columns of white stone frame a porch and contrast with the stucco in original condition, which was never painted and resembles red stone. The ground-floor windows, each under a rounded arch filled with a shell, have unusual wrought iron sashes with brass and copper mouldings. Three horizontal oval windows light the attic storey.

The fine interior includes a delightful octagonal breakfast room – the Birdcage Room – painted in Trompe l'Oeil to resemble the interior of a cage, with views of a garden through the creeper-clad

bamboo bars.

The house was used as a hospital in First World War, then as a convalescent home from 1921. It was closed in 1977 and left derelict until sold to the Priory Hospital Group in 1985, when an award winning restoration with sympathetic rear extension was carried out.

(Above) **Lodge to Grovelands Park,** The Bourne, corner Queen Elizabeth Drive. 1800. *John Nash*. Listed Grade II.

Small single-storey lodge to Grovelands House of stucco with quoins. Not in the hands of the Priory Hospital and sadly much neglected.

The pair of early C19 gun posts outside the gate are separately listed Grade II as are the walls, gates and railings.

Southgate House, High Street. C18.
Listed Grade II*.
Built as a Neoclassical villa in the late C18 and
owned by the Walker family from 1840 to 1922,
then sold to the Middlesex County Council, the
building housed Minchenden School from 1924.
It is now known as the Minchenden Building and
is part of Southgate College.

Segmental flight of six steps with side walls
bearing lamp-holders leads up to a curved segmental porch with four Tuscan columns and a wrought
iron balcony (illustrated left). Second bay from
left, a full height round bow having three sash
windows with glazing bars on each floor. First and
third bays have stone-fronted Venetian windows in
round arched recesses. Stone area wall with cast
iron railings at intervals.

Inside, an elliptical entrance hall and a stairwell
having one end rounded with niches.

The building has a strong similarity to Millfield
House.

Avington Cottage, 117 High Street. C19. Listed Grade II
Two-storey weatherboarded cottage, probably once a stable block. Left part has low pitched hipped roof; right part, possibly an extension, has a crude parapet. First-floor sash windows with glazing bars. On ground floor a late C19 three-light sash window and a six-panel door with modern garage doors at right.

107 & 109 High Street. C18. Listed Grade II.
An altered three-storey, five-bay building with blind central windows. The main block in stock brick, with parapet front and with hipped slate roof. Gauged brick arches to late C19 sash windows. No. 107 has external louvred shutters. Stuccoed ground floor with C19 bay windows, No. 107 square, No. 109 canted. Both houses have several extensions.

111-113 High Street, Southgate

Minchenden Lodge, Blagdens Close.
Listed Local Interest.

An altered and much restored building now used as a centre for the elderly.

(Opposite, top) **Croft Cottage No. 111, Holcolme House No. 113, Avington No. 115, High Street.** C18. Listed Grade II.

A symmetrical composition in stock brick with later additions of various periods. A central three-storey block (No. 113) and two-storey side blocks each with three upper sash windows with glazing bars. Parapet fronts and hipped roofs. No. 111 has old pantiles, No. 113 has modern pantiles and No. 115 modern tiles. Gauged flat brick arches to sash windows with glazing bars. Reeded door-cases with cornice hoods.

Ellington Court, High Street, Southgate. 1937. *Frederick Gibberd.* Unlisted.

Note the subtle avant-garde features, including the cantilevered porches, in this three-storey block of service flats, with projecting rear balconies overlooking the Walker cricket ground.

Nos. 5 & 7 High Street, Southgate. Listed Local Interest.

A pair of small cottages. Note the attractive glazing bar arrangement to the windows on No. 7.

The Southgate Beaumont (formerly Arnos Grove), 15 Cannon Hill. 1723. Listed Grade II*. The central section of this seven-window, three-storey brown brick house with red brick dressings, was built as a family mansion for James Colebrook. The interior was altered by Sir Robert Taylor in 1765 to whom the internal plaster decorations are attributed. In 1777 was sold to the Walker family. The original house now forms the central portion of a large Georgian type C20 block, in red brick. A modern tetrastyle portico has been added to the central entrance. The old part has a good green slate roof and much original woodwork.

Internally there is a very fine stair with Lanscroon mural depicting the Triumph of Julius Caesar, of similar date (1723) to that which was in Broomfield House. A handsome back room is completely decorated in the Adam style and there is another similar smaller room. Lamps on the entrance driveway came from the Wembley exhibition of 1924.

The building was extended in 1928 as offices of the North Metropolitan Electricity Supply Company and called Northmet House. Later transferred to Legal & General Insurance, it has since undergone further adaptation, with the addition of outbuildings, to become the Beaumont Nursing Care Centre.

Old House, 2 The Green. C18. Listed Grade II Pleasing C18 house with mid C19 front of two storeys facing onto the Green, with two leaded dormers and basement. The fairly high pitched slated roof has a narrow eaves cornice with flat modillions. Sash windows with glazing bars, those on ground floor tripartite. Three steps to six-panel door with radial fanlight. Reproduction open-pedimented doorcase on free-standing Tuscan columns. Cast iron railings to area and steps.

Essex House No. 4 and Arnoside House No. 5
The Green. 1720. Listed Grade II*.
Handsome pair of houses each three storeys and basement. Purple/red brick; magnificent design with rusticated brick quoins of dressed stone at corners of buildings. Mullioned cornice of bright red brick and parapet above. Gauged segmental brick arches to sash windows with glazing bars.

Four stone steps, with wrought iron handrails, to paired doors of eight panels (now top glazed) in moulded architraves. Carved ornamental brackets support cornice hoods broken back in centre. Fine Baroque gate-piers with urns, original railings and gates. Once used as a schoolroom – note bell on front parapet.

Arnoside Cottage,
5 The Green. 1715.
Listed Grade II.
Largely restored coach
house building in multi-
coloured stock brick
with hipped tiled roof.
Modern sash and
casement windows.

Essex Coach House,
No. 3 The Green. C18.
Listed Grade II (Group
Value)
Coach house building in
multi-coloured stock brick
with hipped roof, end-on
to the road. Forms a
group with Essex House,
Arnoside, Arnoside
Cottage and the forecourt
railings and gates.

Christ Church, Waterfall Road. 1862-3. *Sir Giles Gilbert Scott* Listed Grade C. Large Gothic building with impressive tower and spire. Nave, aisles, chancel with shorter aisles. Coursed rubble with freestone dressings. Gables over aisle windows. Spacious interior with five-bay nave and tall arcade. Carved reredos and sedilia in varied marbles. Handsome marble font. Early C18 monumental wall slabs from an older church on the same site, the Weld Chapel built in 1615. The church contains magnificent stained glass supplied by William Morris & Co to designs by Burne-Jones and Rossetti.
The walls along the north and east sides of the churchyard are also listed.

(Opposite, top) **Nos. 23 and 26-32** (Consec). **The Green.** C18. M*ichael Searles.* Listed Grade II. A picturesque feature of The Green listed as a group with Ye Olde Cherry Tree. Nos 23 and 26 of yellow stock brick, the others all painted stucco. Sixteen windows, sashes with glazing bars where original. Parapet. Mansard old tiled roof with ten segmental topped dormer windows. Coach arch between Nos. 24 and 26, the upper floor with large four-light mullioned and transomed windows in segmental reeded recess. Raised parapet over the gable top containing semi-circular window. Ground floor with various C19-style shop fronts of village character.

Renovated in 1981 to the architect's original design.

(Opposite, bottom) **Sanford House No. 38 and Norbury House No. 39** The Green. C18. Listed Grade II
Pair of tall stock brick town houses with parapet front, each three storeys, attic and basement built 1775-6 for Richard Goad, a local landowner. Eight steps lead to six-panel doors in panelled reveals, the doorcases with attached Egyptian columns, entablatures and open pediments over fanlights. Slated mansard roof with dormers. Projecting C19 full-height outer canted bays. Sash windows, the inner ones original with glazing bars. **Norbury House** has additional two-storey north wing with original Venetian window on first floor, later Venetian window on ground floor, and modern projecting surgery entrance. Now converted into flats.

Nos. 23-32 The Green, Southgate

Sanford House and Norbury House

Nos. 40 (Ash Lodge) and 41 The Green. C18. Listed Local Interest.

Two complementary cottages. Ash Lodge, with a Georgian fanlight, was used by Southgate local Board of Health in the early 1800s and has a blue plaque depicting its subsequent use as the first offices of Southgate UDC.

Ye Olde Cherry Tree Inn, The Green. C17. Listed Grade II.

One of Enfield's many listed pubs, a happy mixture of development from C17-C20. Originally a coaching inn at the centre of the old village of Southgate, it is now composed of three widely varying blocks of buildings. North to south; early C19 archway to stables with assembly room over brick-built carriageway and side entrance via an iron stairway.

Next comes an attached early C18 yellow brick two-storey house with eaves cornice screened by a wooden frieze and red tiled room with dormers. The lower storey south end has a Tudor style porch and gable added in 1923. Original timber framing is visible from the inside. At the side (in the Mall) the C19 façade joins late C17 or early C18 weatherboarded building on a brick base.

Nos. 6 & 6A Cannon Hill,
Early C19. Listed Grade II.
Originally known as Cannon
Hall, a yellow brick villa with a
low pitched hipped slated roof
and eaves soffit and first-floor
stucco band. Round bow on
ground floor right. Casement
windows, with louvred shutters,
to the north half of the building and sash windows on the
mid C19 two-storey addition.

The Coach House, 4 Cannon Hill, Early C19.
Listed Grade II
Weatherboarded two-storey ranch style building
with projecting wings at either side and an irregular arrangement of windows to first floor. Modern
casements and front door.

Telephone Box K6 type Cannon Hill. *Sir Giles
Gilbert Scott*. 1930s. Listed Local Interest. (Not
illustrated)
The classic K6 phone box was designed in 1935 by
Sir Giles Gilbert Scott. Earlier boxes, known as K2
and by the same designer, were squat-looking with
18 square windows on each of three sides.

The Hermitage, 2 Cannon Hill. Early C19. Listed Grade II.

Thatched cottage orné with ornamental barge-boards to the gables and dormers. Note dripmoulds over the Gothic doorway and the first-floor windows.

Arnos Grove Station, Bowes Road. 1932. *Charles Holden*. Listed Grade II. Probably the best of the Piccadilly line stations to Cockfosters from Bounds Green (all listed and all by Charles Holden). Simple rationalisation influenced by Scandinavian architectural design. Part of the very high quality of design of London Transport in the 1930s with fine attention to detail. Concrete roof, with central glazed drum, radiates from a central sixteen-sided pillar with the original ticket office.

Arnos Pool and Library,
Bowes Road. 1939. *Curtis &
Burchett.* Listed Grade II.
Elegant brick and concrete
buildings by MCC architects.
An oriel window lights the
curved staircase to the library
on the first floor. Forms a
group with the adjoining clinic
building.

Arnos Pool

Arnos Library

**Bowes Road Junior & Infant
School,** Bowes Road, 1901,
Henry William Dobb, Listed
Grade II.
A three-storey building built for
Edmonton Board Schools in
stock brick, red brick and
terracotta with stone dressings.
Tall central bell turret with
faceted spire and weathervane.
The architect, Henry Dobb
lived in Church Street, Edmon-
ton although he was born in
Rotherham.

Palmers Green

The Edwardian houses covering most of Palmers Green were built on fields which once formed part of extensive estates such as Grovelands, Broomfield, Bowes Manor and The Lodge. Until the Grovelands estate was broken up in 1902, the local countryside was dotted with a few hamlets centred on the pubs and road junctions: the old Fox pub, Fox Lane/Hazelwood Lane/Green Lanes, Fox Lane/Bourne Hill (an area known as Clappers Green) and a small settlement (Bowes) round the Cock Tavern.

Palmers Green Station, which was opened by the Great Northern Railway in 1871, was surrounded by open fields for thirty years until the opulent Old Park estate was built on part of the Grovelands land. The broad roads of this estate between Fox Lane and Aldermans Hill, lined with lime trees and London planes, are notable for their finely-detailed houses.

Similar, but less grand, developments rapidly followed: Hazelwood Park estate (1903) between Hedge Lane and Hazelwood Lane, Clappers Green Farm estate (1908) between Fox Lane and Bourne Hill, and The Lodge estate (1911) between Hazelwood Lane and Oakthorpe Road.

Shops and churches were established to cater for the needs of the rapidly expanding suburb. Green Lanes was graced by St John's (1904-9) and St Monica's Roman Catholic Church (1914); Fox Lane by both Congregationalist and Presbyterian churches.

Development, halted by the First World War, resumed in the 1920s and continued until the mid 1930s, when only a few plots of land remained vacant.

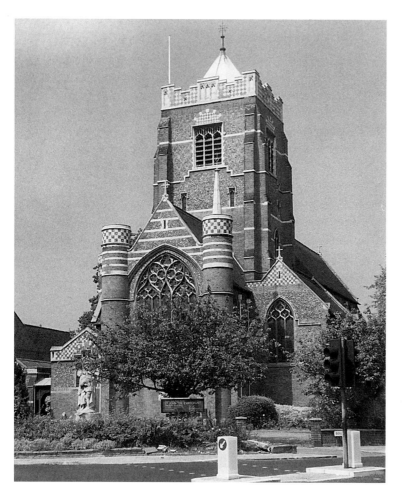

St John the Evangelist, Green Lanes/Bourne Hill. 1904-9.
John Oldrid Scott.
Listed Grade B
Strikingly decorative exterior involving imaginative use of flint rubble and panelling above lower parts in red brick. Flint panelling in peaks of gables and on parapet of tower, also on the two round turrets. Both originally bore a copper spirelet, but only one has survived. Flamboyant traceries on east window, clerestory and aisle windows. Richly varied interior with good stained glass, some by *Morris & Co.*

St John's Church Hall, Bourne Hill. 1908
J. S. Alder. Listed Grade B.
(Not illustrated)
Built in materials to match the church, with a small turret. The Vicarage to the west of the church is also by *J. S. Alder*, 1909.

National Westminster Bank, 288 Green Lanes. 1913 *Arthur Sykes.* Listed Grade II
Accomplished essay in early C20 'Banker's Georgian' style (which was to become extremely popular in the 1920s and 30s) in red brick, with superb rusticated keyed brick arches to ground floor. Sash windows and rusticated quoins to first floor, topped by dentilled cornice. Above the cornice the formality gives way to Arts & Craft-style leanings with a tiled, hipped roof and a tall, commanding chimney stack. Two-storey wing to the rear (Lodge Drive) is also Arts & Crafts style, with a projecting semicircular turret in the centre, topped by a tiled conical roof.

The Fox, Green Lanes/Fox Lane. 1904. Unlisted. (Not illustrated)
Superb, exuberant Edwardian pub on a prominent corner site. Red brick, gloriously detailed with faux-vernacular elements: stone-mullioned windows, projecting half-timbered gables on third storey and band of pargetting between first and second storeys. Circular turret to corner.

Shops, Green Lanes (west side between Aldermans Hill/Devonshire Road.) 1909-13. *Arthur Sykes.* Unlisted. (Not illustrated)
A welcome contrast to the comparatively arid monotony of the shop buildings immediately opposite. Though marred by years of grime and a jumbled array of late C20 shopfronts to the ground floor, this large parade is nevertheless impressive. Red brick, stone-mullioned leaded casement windows, dormers and chimney stacks to tiled roof, with the elevation broken up at intervals by projections and, opposite the junction with Lodge Drive, a huge Voyseyesque gable.

Truro House, 176 Green Lanes. Early C19. Listed Grade II.

One of the few remnants of rural Palmers Green which survived the Edwardian onslaught, Truro House is set in grounds backing onto the New River. Breach the boundary wall and you could almost be in France or northern Italy. This early C19 country villa has a continental flavour, courtesy of its shallow pitched roof, green-painted louvred shutters, prostyle Corinthian porch and Ionic bow window to south garden side. The impressive interior is a curious mix of French Baroque and English Tudor. The hallway and several rooms have dark oak panelling with stained-glass leaded windows and chimney-pieces which possibly predate the house.

The boundary walls, gate piers and wrought iron gates are listed Grade II.

Victoria Cottage, 84 Hoppers Road and **Roses Cottage,** 86 Hoppers Road. Early C19. Listed Local Interest.

Two double-fronted cottages in whitewashed brick with attractive wooden shutters to ground floor.

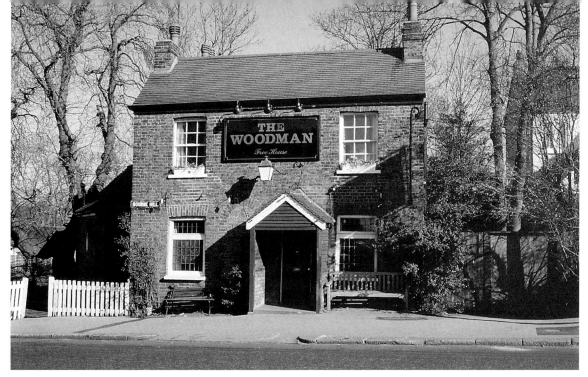

The Woodman, Bourne Hill. Late C18/early C19. Listed Local Interest.

Together with the surviving skeleton of the former cattle pound across the road, this old pub (licensed 1868) is a reminder of when Bourne Hill was a winding country lane. Originally two smaller cottages, now altered and enlarged.

Menlow Lodge (part of former Southgate County School), Fox Lane. 1910 *H. G. Crothall.* Listed Grade II. (Group Value)

Built in the free Baroque style favoured by the MCC architect: stone window surrounds, steep roof, inset brick quoins at the corners. Converted into flats in 1989.

Broomfield House, Broomfield Lane. Various periods from C16-early C20. Listed Grade II*.
The ruins of this splendid mansion stand as a gaunt reproach to successive local authority administrations which lacked the will to restore the house after it was gutted by fire in 1984. Subsequent fires in 1993 and 1994 increased the dilapidation.

Expanded over the centuries from a timber-framed farmhouse, Broomfield House and much of its surrounding park was bought by Southgate Council in 1902. The park was opened to the public the following year. Southgate County School used the house from 1909-10; it later became a health clinic, museum and café. The interior features, especially several panelled rooms, suffered badly in the fires, but efforts were made to salvage the splendid early C18 staircase and the magnificent Baroque mural paintings on the staircase walls and ceiling. Dated 1726, by Gerard Lanscroon, the remains of the murals which had been restored shortly before the fire, are in a council store.

Broomfield House before the fire

East Wall, of Broomfield Park including attached **Garden House** and **Stable Block.** Mid C16 and C18. Listed Grade II*.

South Walls, of Broomfield Park and **inner garden walls** (C16/earlyC17) and west walls of park (C18) listed Grade II. The grounds have been included as Grade II in the Department of the Environment register of historic parks and gardens. Their layout, including the three ponds which still exist, is shown on Rocque's 1754 map of Middlesex.

Coach House and outbuildings to south-east of Broomfield House, listed Local Interest. (Not illustrated)

St Michael-at-Bowes, Whittington Road N22. 1988.

The original Gothic-style church by Sir George Gilbert Scott was demolished in 1987 and replaced by a modern design, given character by an angular, slate-covered roofline. A projection from the roof facing the road bears a large symbol of an angel carrying a cross, an ornate flourish which relieves an otherwise hard-edged, geometric building.

Hadley Wood, Cockfosters & The Ridgeway

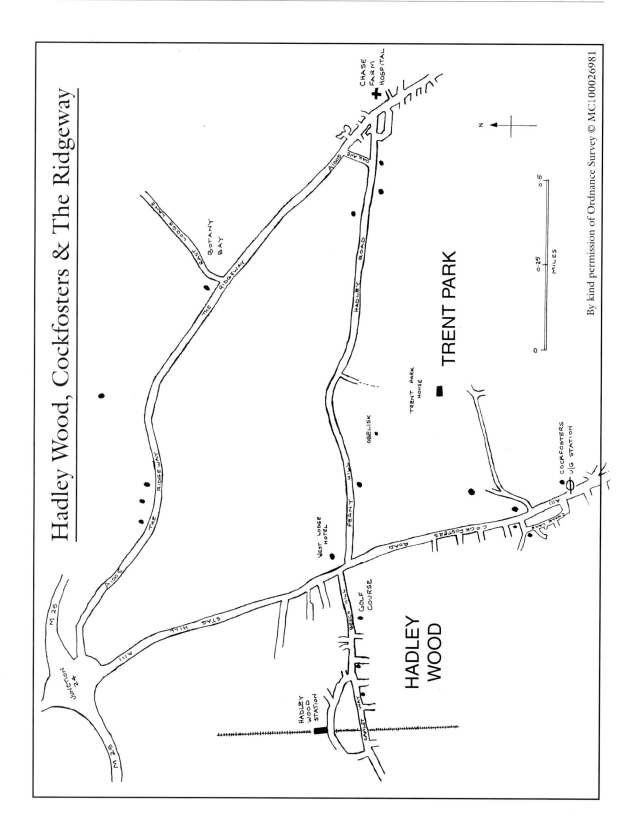

TRENT PARK

HADLEY WOOD

CHASE FARM HOSPITAL

BOTANY BAY

TRENT PARK HOUSE

OBELISK

WEST LODGE HOTEL

GOLF COURSE

HADLEY WOOD STATION

COCKFOSTERS U/G STATION

JUNCTION 24

THE RIDGEWAY

EAST LODGE LANE

OAK AVE

HADLEY ROAD

FERNY HILL

COCKFOSTERS ROAD

STAG HILL

BEECH HILL

CAMLET WAY

M 25

A1005

A111

MILES
0   0·25   0·5

By kind permission of Ordnance Survey © MC100026981

Hadley Wood, Cockfosters & The Ridgeway

The countryside in the north-west corner of Enfield formed part of the ancient Enfield Chase, and the rolling fields on each side of The Ridgeway are still known by that name. Acknowledged as one of the finest landscapes in the Greater London area, Enfield Chase was identified as Heritage Land and an Area of Special Character in 1988.

Geoffrey de Mandeville converted Enfield Wood (part of the old forest of Middlesex) into a chase in about 1136. Covered mainly by woodland and scrub, it later became a royal hunting ground. When the Chase was enclosed in 1777 several roads, including World's End Lane, were laid out and mansions were built by the owners of the newly-created estates: Beech Hill Park (now Hadley Wood Golf Club) and Trent Place, which after enlargement by successive owners became known as Trent Park.

Cockfosters, situated between the two, developed as a hamlet for the estate workers. Christ Church was built in 1839 to serve the cottages in Chalk Lane and Cockfosters Road, but the area scarcely changed until the Piccadilly Line reached Cockfosters in 1933. A frenzy of development followed until, on the eve of war, green belt legislation halted the onrush of suburbia at Cockfosters Road.

The land now covered by Hadley Wood was nearly all owned by Charles Jack, who acquired the freehold of Beech Hill Park estate and some agricultural holdings in the 1870s, a time of agricultural depression. Jack persuaded the Great Northern Railway to open a station in Hadley Wood in 1885 and within ten years some 50 houses had been built in the newly created Crescent East and Crescent West. Lancaster Avenue and Crescent Way followed before the First World War intervened. Between the wars Hadley Wood almost trebled its size to 300 houses, but only limited development has taken place since 1950.

Hadley Wood Station was rebuilt in 1959 and the line was electrified in 1976.

Hadley Wood Golf Club House, Beech Hill. Late C18. Listed Grade II.

Originally Russell Mansion, built for Francis Russell the Duchy Surveyor after the Chase enclosure of 1777. Yellow stock brick, of two storeys incorporating an older rear section. To the front, seven windows and four Doric pilasters defuse the centre and support an entablature. Gauged brick arches serve the sash windows and a prostyle Doric porch with dentil cornice provides front access. Single-storey side pavilions, added in the C19, are of stuccoed brickwork. Each has three round-headed casement windows.

Internally, an impressive hall with Corinthian pilasters and detailed plasterwork, curved staircase with detailed handrail.

To the rear the early C19 **stable range** (also listed) is on two floors. All the ground-floor openings are round-headed. Later service additions on right.

Stable Block, Hadley Wood Golf Club

Camlet House, 53 Beech Hill. 1875-80. *F. Lambert.* Listed Grade II.

In Greek style, two storeys in six large bays with decorated square columns to porch and similar decorated piers to tripartite windows. The concrete block walls and later brick additions are stucco-covered, the front parapets hiding shallow pitched slate roofs. In the Twenties this was the home of Sir Nigel Gresley, chief mechanical engineer to the LNER, who designed *Mallard* the world's fastest steam locomotive.

No. 83 Camlet Way (see page 170)

Nos. 89-91 Camlet Way

Nos. 83, 87, 89/91 Camlet Way. Late C19. Listed Grade II. These four houses were estate cottages serving the now demolished Broadgates Manor. They stand on a roadway (Camlet Way and Beech Hill) defined by Francis Russell, the Duchy Surveyor. **No. 83** is a tall, imposing cottage-style house in red brick with fishscale tile-hanging to first floor. Steep pitched plain tiled roof with timbered and stuccoed gables, detailed brick chimneys, all in Vernacular Revival style. **No. 87** similar in style though less lofty. **Nos 89/91** slightly varied style but similar materials, forming two semi-detached units.

Dacre Cottage, Chalk Lane. mid C18. Listed Local Interest. Overlooking the sports ground and once very central to the heart of old Cockfosters, which has records back to 1372. An extended two-storey brick-walled structure with slate roof.

Cockfosters LRT Station, Cockfosters Road. 1933. *Charles Holden*. Listed Grade II. Brick and concrete entrance to the long, low station building with cantilevered canopy extending over the whole width, forming a clerestory above the main track. Original light fittings.

Platform Detail, Cockfosters Station

Nos. 325-335 Cockfosters Road, Mid C19. Listed Grade II.
Terrace of six two-storey estate cottages with brick façades. Note the shared gabled porches below blank windows.

(Opposite) **Trent Park House,** Cockfosters Road. 1895. Listed Grade II.
Part of Middlesex University, a farm, a country park and a golf course make up the 950-acre Trent Park estate, which was formed as part of the enclosures on Enfield Chase in 1777. It was acquired by Sir Richard Jebb, a royal physician who was knighted after saving the life of the Duke of Gloucester at Trent in the Tyrol. Jebb built a modest villa which was greatly extended and altered in 1895. The house underwent another transformation between 1926-31 when Sir Philip Sassoon MP commissioned *Philip Tilden* to enlarge and recase the building in early Georgian style, with red brick walls, stone quoins and a balustraded parapet. A fine entrance hall and staircase, and interesting decorative features including murals by *Rex Whistler* survive in the house, where Sassoon entertained the Prince of Wales (later Edward VIII), Winston Churchill and other notables in the 1930s.

Ancillary buildings include an **Orangery** (listed Grade II) designed by *Reginald Cooper* with water garden, a pergola known as **Wisteria Walk** (listed Grade II) with Italian columns of pink marble, and C18 delicate **wrought iron gates.** Some fine listed C17 **statues, obelisks** and a variety of **sculptures** add interest to the splendid grounds, which are owned by the London Borough of Enfield.

The late C19 **west entrance gateway** in Cockfosters Road and the flanking battered **stone bollards** with chamfered angles and ogee domed tops, are also listed Grade II.

Trent Park

The Orangery, Trent Park

*Wisteria Walk,
Trent Park*

Statue of Venus, Trent Park

The Obelisk, Trent Park

Barn, Ferny Hill Farm, Listed Local Interest. (Not illustrated)
The ravages of time have been repaired in modern materials but the old timber frame and timber trusses of the barn can be seen in the working farm building.

West Lodge Park Hotel, Ferny Hill. C18. Listed Local Interest.
Built on the site of one of the early C16 lodges for the underkeepers of Enfield Chase, the two-storey south wing dates from the C18. Spacious entrance hall with C18 staircase. Grounds include the Beale Arboretum with hundreds of fine specimen trees.

Wolverton, Hadley Road

Pumping Station, Hadley Road

(Opposite, top) **Wolverton,** Hadley Road. C20. Listed Local Interest.

Imposing country house, brick-built, two storeys plus dormers, with stone quoins and part vertical tiling, Rear elevation enlivened with balconies and balustrades, An interesting stable block to the front requires renovation.

(Opposite, bottom) **Pumping Station,** Hadley Road. 1903. Listed Local Interest.

A massive structure mainly of engineering brick up to a pitched, slated roof. Internally with glazed tile walls. Originally a coal-fired station drawing from a well, but now a diesel-powered booster station for the local community supplies.

Vicarage Farm Cottages, Hadley Road. C20. Listed Local Interest.

Two traditional farm workers' cottages, brick-built and rendered, under slated roofs.

North Lodge (St John's Senior School), The Ridgeway. Late C18. Listed Grade II.
Now in use as a private school, North Lodge was the seat of the Gundry family and was for a time occupied by the Marchioness of Ely. The rendered façades serving the two storeys rise to a balustraded, slated roof with dormer windows. A columned portico serves the front door which is central below a pediment. Interior features include a fine C18 fireplace.

(Opposite, top) **Holly Hill Farmhouse,** The Ridgeway, Botany Bay. Mid C19. Listed Grade II. Wide, two-storey villa under pitched slate roof. Gauged brick flat arches to sash windows. Rounded niched entrance with double door and patterned fanlight.

(Opposite, bottom) **The Hollies,** The Ridgeway, Botany Bay. C19. Listed Local Interest.
Attractive two storey, two-section country house with rendered brick walls and hipped slated roof. Rear additions, in plain brick and slate, housed stables, etc.

Holly Hill Farmhouse, The Ridgeway

The Hollies, The Ridgeway

Water Tower,
The Ridgeway. 1913.
Listed Local Interest.
Octagonal red brick
structure with detailed
corbelling and
crenellated brick and
stone coping.

Notable Architects & Artists

Alder, John Samuel (1845-1919). Born in Birmingham, the son of a builder. Articled to a firm of architects in Hereford and Malvern; moved to London and commenced practice in 1887. Responsible for numerous buildings especially churches, in North London and Middlesex. *1906, Holy Trinity; Winchmore Hill, and St Stephen's, Bush Hill Park. 1907, Charles Lamb Institute, Church Street, Edmonton.* Also *Church Halls at St John's Palmers Green, St Michael's, Edmonton, St Mary's, Edmonton,* and others.

Brooks, James (1825-1901). Son of a Berkshire farmer. Entered Royal Academy School of Architecture 1847; set up own practice 1851. Built numerous London churches, especially in the East End, using early 13th century style and stock brick, his favourite material, as demonstrated in *St Luke's Church* and *Vicarage, Browning Road, 1899.*

Burne-Jones, Sir Edward (1833-98). British pre-Raphaelite painter, inspired by Arthurian legends and Greek myths, renowned for glowing colours and purity of line. *Stained-glass windows, Christ Church, Waterfall Road, 1876, 1885 and 1899.*

Butterfield, William (1814-1900). One of nine children, father a chemist in the Strand, London. Apprenticed to a builder then articled to an architect before setting up practice in Lincolns Inn. Deeply religious member of Anglican High Church. All Saints, Margaret Street (1849) his first church building, was his masterpiece. *1883, St Mary Magdalene, Windmill Hill,* with typically handsome interior, and *Vicarage (Ridge End)* to match the church.

Caröe, William Douglas 1857-1938). Born in Liverpool, the son of a Danish consul, and educated at Trinity College, Cambridge. Worked mainly for the Ecclesiastical Commissioners, building many churches in and around London, mostly in Gothic style but with a very individual Arts & Crafts influence, eg *St Aldhelm, Silver Street, Edmonton, 1903.* Other work included University College. Cardiff and LCC flats behind Millbank.

Gibberd, Sir Frederick (1908-84). Winner of numerous Civic Trust awards. Early work includes *Ellington Court, High Street, Southgate, 1936.* Architect/planner for Harlow New Town, best known for Heathrow control tower and first passenger terminal, Regents Park Mosque and Liverpool's Roman Catholic Cathedral.

Heaps, S. A. London Transport architect who worked closely with Holden.

Holden, Charles Henry (1875-1960). Born in Bolton. In 1898 worked under and was influenced by Arts & Crafts architect C. R. Ashbee at Royal Academy School of Architecture. Later a partner in Adams, Holden and Pearson. Designed Rhodesia House in the Strand, stations on Northern Line extension to Morden, London Transport building in Broadway SW1 and (1928) the circular concourse at Piccadilly underground station. Between *1930-34, Piccadilly Line extension to Cockfosters.* Enfield has the three best stations: *Arnos Grove, Southgate and Oakwood.*

Lanscroon, Gerard. Flemish artist who worked under Antonio Verrio in 1678 on the state apartments at Windsor Castle and also at Hampton Court. *1723, series of grand Baroque murals at Arnos Grove (Southgate House)* depicting life of Julius Caesar. *1726, classical murals on staircase walls and ceiling at Broomfield House* (seriously damaged by fire).

Mackmurdo, Arthur Heygate (1851-1942). Born in Church Street Edmonton, son of a wealthy Scottish businessman who married into the D'Oyley Carte family. Educated at Felsted School, Essex, he was apprenticed to T. Charfield Clarke then worked under the Gothicist James Brooks. Travelled to Italy with Ruskin in 1874 and later, through his cousin Richard D'Oyley Carte, made contact with the aesthetic movement. In 1882 founded the Century Guild, a group of architects, designers and artists inspired by Ruskin and William Morris. Moved to Enfield the following year and established a craft workshop. Built *Brooklyn, Private Road, 1887* and a few other houses, notable for their original, elegantly simple design. A pioneer of Art Nouveau, Mackmurdo exerted considerable influence on contemporary artists and architects, including C. F. A. Voysey, through his numerous designs, pamphlets and books published by the

A. H. Mackmurdo (standing) photographed in the 1880s with his mother at Halcyon, the house he designed for her in Private Road, Enfield. Seated left is Herbert Horne, who was articled to Mackmurdo's architectural practice and was co-founder with him of The Century Guild.

Century Guild.

Maufe, Sir Edward (1883-1974). Noted designer of modern churches in simplified Gothic style with Swedish influence, eg St Columba's, Pont Street. Major work, the brick-built Guildford Cathedral (1932-66). Chief architect to Commonwealth War Graves Commission 1941-69, designed the memorial at Runnymead. Built the Festival Theatre, Chichester after the war, rebuilt Grays Inn and Middle Temple. *St Alphege, Hertford Road, 1957.*

Morris, William (1834-96). Craftsman and poet who revolutionised the art of house furnishing and decoration, exerting a strong influence on architects and designers. In 1861, founded his own design and manufacturing company with pre-Raphaelite friends. Remarkable *windows* by Morris

& Co. with some designed by Wm Morris (including possible self-portrait as St Matthew) *Christ Church, Waterfall Road, 1862-1913. Windows* by Morris & Co., *St John the Evangelist, Palmers Green.*

Mylne, Robert (1733-1811). Scottish architect, planned Gloucester and Berkeley Ship Canal and the Eau Brink Cut for fen drainage at King's Lynn. Appointed assistant engineer to New River Company 1767, later chief engineer. Built *Bush Hill Sluice and Clarendon Arch.* Was succeeded as chief engineer by his son, Robert Chadwell Mylne.

Nash, John (1752-1835). Son of a Lambeth millwright and a Welsh mother, trained under Palladian architect Sir Robert Taylor but by 1780 was on his own, building speculative stucco-fronted terraces, then a novelty. Bankrupted in 1783 he retired to relatives in Wales but bounced back, in partnership with landscape gardener Humphry Repton, to design a huge output of country houses in every imaginable style, the finest in the London area being *Southgate Grove (Grovelands) 1797*. Greatest work was layout of Regent's Park and Regent Street (from 1811). Also planned Trafalgar Square, built Clarence House, Carlton House Terrace and Suffolk Square

St Aubyn, James Piers (1915-95). Born in Powick, Worcestershire, where his father was the vicar, soon moving to a parish near Penzance, Cornwall. Articled to a practice in Gloucester, moved to London in 1851 and was appointed Surveyor of the Middle Temple. Restored Temple Church, 1861-3. In 1878 carried out extensions to the castle at St Michael's Mount. Built or restored churches all over the country, especially Devon and Cornwall. Locally, *St John's, Clay Hill, 1857 and the Vicarage (now Glenwood House) and alterations to the choir, St Andrew's, Enfield, 1853*.

Scott, Sir George Gilbert (1811-78). Son of a village clergyman in Buckinghamshire, had little formal education, was articled to an obscure London architect, then teamed up with W. B. Moffatt to build workhouses. First important building (1843) Royal Wanstead School, E11. Went on alone to build numerous churches in a mixed Anglo-French High Gothic style. *1862, Christ Church, Waterfall Road*. Secular buildings include St Pancras Station and Hotel (1865) and the Albert Memorial (1864).

Scott, John Oldrid (1841-1913). Second son of Sir G. G. Scott, whose practice he inherited. Built or worked on many fine churches in north London including *St John the Evangelist, Green Lanes/ Bourne Hill.1903*.

Scott, William Gilbee (1857-1930). Lived at Harden House, Waverley Road, Enfield, and was founder shareholder of Enfield Golf Club, 1902. Was responsible for the *layout of the Old Park estate from 1880* (Waverley Road, etc). Built up an extensive general practice. Local work included *restoration of All Saints, Edmonton, 1889; Barclays Bank, Enfield Town, 1897; Baptist Church, Cecil Road, 1925*.

Voysey, Charles Francis Annesley (1857-1941). Architect and designer of numerous country houses, often with roughcast exteriors and low, comfortable rooms, influenced by William Morris and Mackmurdo.

Glossary

1 Architrave surround
2 Balustraded parapet
3 Corinthian entablature
4 Dentilled cornice
5 Double hung sash window
6 Double doors with four moulded panels
7 Glazing bars
8 Hipped roof
9 Keystone
10 Projecting wing
11 Sepentine open pediment
12 Stone quoins
13 String course or band

Aisle. Space parallel to, but separated by pillars from, the nave or choir of a church.

Apse. Semicircular or polygonal end, usually to a church or chapel.

Architrave. The lowest of the three main parts of an entablature (*qv*). The moulded frame surrounding a door or window.

Ashlar. Masonry blocks hewn to even faces and square edges, laid in horizontal courses with vertical joints.

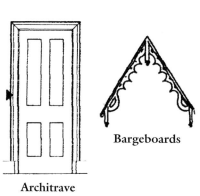

Architrave

Bargeboards

Attic. Room within the roof space of a house.

Balustrade. Series of short posts or pillars supporting a rail or coping.

Banded Column. See column.

Bargeboards. Projecting boards, often carved or fretted, fixed under the incline of a gable, hiding the ends of the horizontal roof timbers.

Bay Window. Window of one or more storeys projecting from

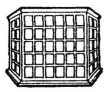

Bay window (canted)

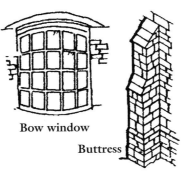

Bow window

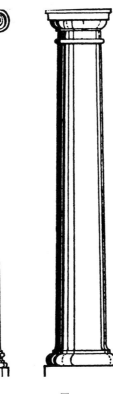

Buttress

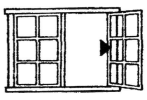

Casement

the face of a house. *Canted*, with straight front and angled sides. *Bow*, curved. *Oriel*, supported by brackets starting above ground level.

Blocking Course. Plain course of stone surmounting the cornice at the top of a building. Also a projecting course of stone or brick at base of a building.

Broach Spire. Octagonal spire with triangular faces, set on a square base.

Buttress. Masonry or brickwork projecting from, or built against, a wall or monument to give additional strength.

Cartouche. Ornamental panel in the form of a scroll, often with ornate frame.

Casement Window. Wooden or metal window hinged at the side.

Chamfer. Surface made when the sharp edge of a wood or stone block is cut away.

Chancel. Part of the east end of a church containing the main altar and reserved for clergy and choir.

Clerestory. Upper stage of the side walls of a church, pierced with windows above the aisle and nave. Also applicable to high-level windows in secular buildings.

Column. Upright member of round section, with shaft, capital and (usually) base, decorated according to accepted classical style. *Corinthian*, fluted shaft, ornate capital with Acanthus leaf carving. *Doric*, fluted shaft, stepped bowl-shape capital. *Ionic*, fluted shaft, scrolled capital. *Tuscan*, plain shaft, bowl-shape capital. *Banded* or *Rusticated*, shaft interrupted by bands of plain or rusticated square blocks.

Coping. Flat or sloping brick or stone capping to protect a wall.

Corbelling. Brick or masonry courses, each projecting beyond the one below, to support a chimney stack, window, etc.

Corinthian Column. See Column.

Cornice. Decorative ornamental moulding between wall and ceiling. Flat-topped ledge with decorated underside projecting along the top of a building, wall, arch, etc. Top projecting section of classical entablature.

Cottage Orné. Artfully rustic building inspired by the late C18/early C19 Picturesque movement.

Crenellation. Parapet with alternate raised portions and indentations; also called battlement.

Crucks. Pairs of long, curved timbers (blades) used as an arch to support the roof timbers and,

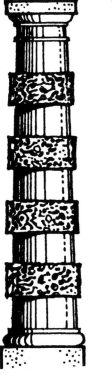

Banded or rusticated column

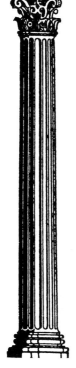

Corinthian column

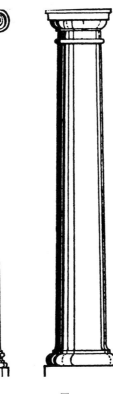

Ionic column

Tuscan column

in timber buildings, as the principal framing for a house. *Upper cruck*, blades rising from a tiebeam to the apex of a roof.

Cupola. Small dome on a round or polygonal base crowning a roof, turret or larger dome.

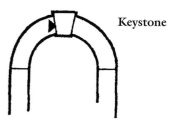
Fanlight

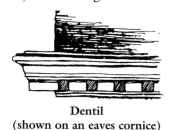

Dentil
(shown on an eaves cornice)

Dentil. Small square block used in series in classical cornices.

Diaper Work. All-over surface decoration of small repeated pattern, usually squares or lozenges.

Doric Column. See Column.

Dormer window

Dormer Window. Window placed vertically in a sloping roof (usually serving a bedroom, hence the name).

Dressings. Stones worked to a finished face, set around an angle, window or other feature.

Eaves. Overhanging edges of a roof.

Entablature. Classical term for the three members (architrave, frieze and cornice) carried horizontally by a wall or column.

Fenestration. The arrangement of windows in a building.

Flêche. Slender spire, usually wood, rising from the ridge of a building.

Frieze. Middle division of an entablature, between the architrave

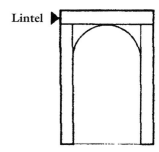
Flemish bond brickwork

and cornice. Decorated horizontal band on an internal wall.

Gable. Triangular part of wall at end of a pitched roof, normally with straight sides. *Dutch gable* has curved sides crowned by a pediment.

Gambrel Roof. See Roof.

Gauged Arches. Soft bricks sawn to shape then rubbed to a precise (gauged) fit, usually round a window or door.

Glazing Bars. Wooden or metal bars separating lights in a window.

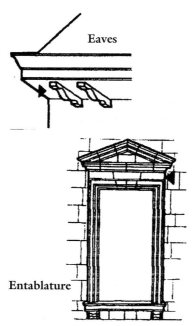
Eaves

Entablature

Hipprd Roof. See Roof.

Impost Course. Projecting bracket-like moulding in a wall, supporting the end of an arch.

Ionic Column. See Column.

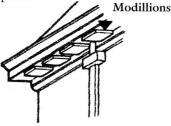

Keystone

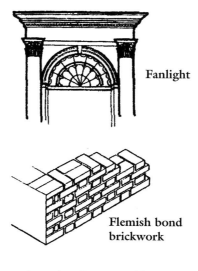

Lintel ▶

Keystone. Central stone in an arch.

Lintel. Horizontal beam of wood or stone bridging an opening.

Lunette. Semicircular window or panel.

Modillions

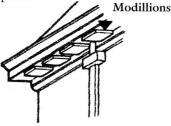

Mansard Roof. See Roof.

Modillions. Small brackets or consoles supporting the underside of a Corinthian or eaves cornice.

Mullion. Vertical upright between window lights.

Nave. Part of a church west of the chancel or crossing, usually flanked by aisles.

Oculus. Circular window or opening.

Ogee. Double curve in shape of S or inverted S.

Oriel Window. See Bay window.
Oversail or Overthrow. System of construction in which the upper storey of a building is thrust out over the lower. Decorative arch between two gate piers or over a wrought iron gate.
Parapet. Low wall to protect a sudden drop. Also used to conceal a roof.
Pargetting. Exterior plaster decoration, usually in relief.
Pavilion. Ornamental building for pleasurable use. Projecting subdivision of a larger building.

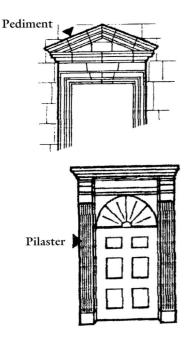

Pediment

Pilaster

Pediment. Low-pitched gable above a portico, door or window.
Pilaster. Shallow, flat column projecting slightly from a wall.
Portico. Large roofed porch supported by columns. *Prostyle* when columns are free-standing.
Quoins. Dressed stones at the corners of a building. *Vermiculated,* with surface to imitate worm-casts.
Rendering. Plastering on an outer wall. *Roughcast,* plaster

mixed with gravel. *Stucco,* fine lime plaster with a smooth surface.
Return. Part which falls away, usually at right angles, from the front of a building.
Reveal. The part of a jamb between the frame of a door or window and a wall.
Roof. *Gambrel* roof has a small gable at the ridge. *Hipped* has sloped instead of vertical ends. *Mansard* has two slopes, the lower being longer and steeper than the upper. *Pent,* sloping in one direction only.

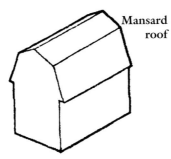

Mansard roof

Rubble. Masonry stones left in a rough state. *Courses,* rough-faced stones laid in a course.
Rustication. Masonry cut in massive blocks and given a rich, bold texture to enhance an exterior wall.
Sash Window. Timber-framed (rarely metal-framed) panes running in vertical grooves.
Sedilla. Seats for clergy on the south side of the chancel.

Quoins

Soffit. Underside of an arch, lintel etc.
Spandrel. Triangular space between an arch and its rectangular frame, or between adjacent arches in an arcade.
Stringing. Projecting horizontal course, usually moulded, in an exterior wall.
Stucco. See Rendering.
Timber Framing. Construction composed of interlocking timber framework with spaces filled in by lath and plaster, wattle and daub or brickwork.
Transom. Horizontal bar separating window lights.
Triglyph. Stylised grooved blocks in a Doric frieze.
Tuscan Column. See Column.
Tympanum. Area within a pediment or between a lintel and the arch above it.

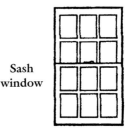

Sash window

Venetian window

Venetian Window. Window with three sections, the central one arched and wider than the others.
Vermiculated. See Rendering.
Voussoirs. Brick or wedge-shaped stones forming an arch.
Weatherboarding. Overlapping horizontal boards covering a wall.

Further Reading & Sources

Brindle, Steven, *Broomfield, an illustrated history of the house and garden.* (Southgate District Civic Trust).

Carter, Valerie, Perryman, Peter & Skilton, Alan. *Enfield's Architectural Heritage,* (Enfield Preservation Society).

Carter, Valerie. *Fighting for the future, the story of Enfield Preservation Society 1936-1996.* (Enfield Preservation Society).

Cherry, Bridget & Pevsner, Nikolaus. *The buildings of England, London 4: North* (Penguin Books).

Dalling, Graham. *Enfield past.* (Historical Publications).

Dalling, Graham. *Southgate and Edmonton past.* (Historical Publications).

Eccleston, Matthew. *Enfield: portrait of a London Borough*

Enfield Preservation Society. *Portrait of Gentleman's Row.*

Gillam, Geoffrey. *Forty Hall.* (Enfield Archaeological Society).

Pam, David. *A history of Enfield.* (Enfield Preservation Society). Three volumes:
> *Volume 1: A parish near London* (Before 1837).
> *Volume 2: A Victorian suburb* (1837-1913).
> *Volume 3: A desirable neighbourhood* (1914-1939).

Pam, David. *The Royal Small Arms Factory, Enfield, and its workers.*

Enfield Preservation Society

Enfield Preservation Society, founded in 1936, has an unrivalled record of vigorous activity in defence of the natural and built environment. Many of the buildings pictured in this book have survived thanks to intervention by EPS. Recent initiatives include the renovation of the New River Loop in Enfield and attempts to form an independant trust to run the house and museum at Forty Hall (in partnership with the LBE) for the benefit of the public.

The EPS is represented on all the relevant consultative bodies set up by the London Borough of Enfield, including the Conservation Advisory Group, Green Belt Forum and Enfield in Bloom. It is affiliated to the Civic Trust, the Society for the Protection of Ancient Buildings, and other national amenity organisations.

Regular meetings, walks and outings are organised for members, who receive a quarterly newsletter. Membership inquiries will be welcomed by the hon. secretary at EPS headquarters: Jubilee Hall, 2 Parsonage Lane, Enfield, Middlesex EN2 OAJ.

Index